CW00863440

Divine Creation

Gali Lucy

Copyright © 2021 Gali Lucy Nadiv

All rights reserved

2nd English Edition 2021 /1st English Edition 2016
Hebrew Edition 2015

Cover design by: Dalit Rahamim

Pictures, illustrations, and cover: Justcolor.net, Pixabay.com
ISBN-13: 9798511026022

Author Website:
www.Gali4u.com

No part of this book may be reproduced, copied, stored or
transmitted in any form by any means - graphic, electronic
or mechanical including photocopying, recording or
information storage and retrieval systems without the prior
written permission of the author. This book and its logo are
trademarks.

The information contained in this book is in no shape or
form a diagnosis, prescription or treatment of any health
disorder whatsoever. This information simply presents a
suggestion or an opinion of the author and should not
replace consultation with a competent healthcare
professional. In the case of any medical, mental or
psychological problem, one must consult proper health care
professionals. The author and the publisher are in no way
liable for any misuse of the material.

Table of Contents

Divine Message 1

All of you shall care for one another and be as one and I shall gather you from the four corners of the world. I shall uplift your souls from the gutters, to lead you from despair and doom, with the ancient knowledge to ' Tikkun Olam', repairing the world.

Righteousness and purity shall cleanse your thirsty souls, to prepare you for the future, teach you the secrets and unite your souls. In the distant future, I shall wash your faces in turbulent oceans, earthquakes, and signs.

This book is for the generations, contains my words. There is no anger, fury, or punishment - all of me is love.

I prayed to God:
"Let me have everything so that I may enjoy life".

& God replied:
"I gave you life - so that you may enjoy everything".

A folk saying

This message was received through channeling.

Divine Message 2

Dearly beloved,

who are asking for assistance and guidance in your lives,
so you may understand where you should turn to next.

Go to the wise and silent person,

who does not ask for alms or provides you with talismans,
who does not walk wearing fine clothes or spends his time
in temples and luxurious buildings.

You will reach that person by word of mouth.
Be wise, go to the modest, quiet, and humble ones.

The words of wisdom of heaven are spoken quietly
with humor and a smile, not with shouting, threats
and intimidation.

Not by might nor by power, but by spirit,
I am the LORD.

This message was received through channeling.

Introduction

This book was written using male pronouns, yet it is intended to apply to both genders. I would like to thank all those who purchased, received, or borrowed this book. Nothing is coincidental!

This book was transferred to me during channeling and typed directly into the computer. It was written to satisfy the public's curiosity with insights and knowledge which my soul has collected through its thousands of incarnations. All that is required of you the reader is curiosity, flexible thinking with a healthy sense of humor, and a willingness to accept new ideas.

Do not believe this book, but find your own truth, because there will never be one truth in order to provide you with a free will to choose.

The purpose of this book:

The contents of this book provide explanations in simple language to the question "Who are we?", as well as other important questions, such as:

• Who is God / *The Creation*, *The Creators*, and *The Created*?

- How was life on Earth and humanity created?
- Why are we here and what is the purpose of humanity?
- What is fate, destiny, and soul?
- What is heaven and hell, and is there life after death?
- What are the rules of the universe?

Before we begin, here are a few basic insights:

- **There never was and never will be a single truth,** because it denies the right to choose. If there was only one truth - you would have been prevented from thinking otherwise; therefore, accept the contents of this book as additional opinions which can enrich the knowledge you already possess.
It is important that you create your own personal opinion and way of thinking, open your mind, and never blindly follow other people's ideas, but research.

- **You are all balls of light,** who borrow a soul from the souls bank and thus breathe life into the body to complete a lesson from a previous life. You are temporary guests inside a human form.

- **Nothing was nor ever will be yours, other than your free will.** Even your soul is not yours, but was lent to you from the soul's bank, in order for you to complete your destiny.

- **Life is like a game of monopoly:**

Each player (a living human being) begins at the starting point (birth) with a backpack (his soul's journey) and a roadmap which contains the player's chosen main lines of his destiny, combined with the soul's secondary lines, which are created by the player during his life.

During this game, the player undergoes changes, buys / sells, builds / separates, ascends / descends, finishes the game's round (dies) and returns to the starting point (the soul 'returns home' to God). Then it starts all over again (the spirit is reborn in a new body or remains as a spirit) with a new roadmap (the lines of destiny) in a new location somewhere on Earth or in some other location in the infinite universe. In your original source you are not a soul, but a ball of light. A soul is inside a living human body and a spirit is when a soul is outside the body.

- **Your aim is to endlessly recreate.**

You are all originally a spirit. You chose to be embodied in **material** living bodies for a short time, in order to testify to the nature of your **soul**:

- Who you are as a spirit.

- The nature of *The Creation*.

- **God can never be ONE!**

The Creation always allows a free choice between at least two options, that's why God is not one but many.

- **No material will make a soul happy for long, only emotions will.**

- **You cannot die.**
You are originally made of spirit which cannot be extinguished. You're all eternal souls.

- *"All is foreseen, but freedom of choice is given".*

A question may come to mind:
"If all is foreseen - then where is the person's choice?"

And the answer is:
"The Creation (God) will never interfere in the human's choice. A divine pattern exists with the main destiny lines of each person, while there is free will to select each move."

For example, imagine driving a vehicle on an existing road which has multiple paths (= all is foreseen), yet **the right to choose** how and where to drive between those paths through interchanges and shortcuts **is given to you,** the driver (= freedom of choice is given).
You can lengthen or shorten your road, but eventually, you will reach the same target foretold.

- **All will happen - only time changes.**

- **All the diseases originate from the soul.**

A spirit cannot be cured using only material; therefore, medicines (drugs) can't cure in the long term, but can only silence the problem, which stems from the person's soul.

- **All religions involve material and violate the free will.**
Spirituality cannot be religious, because a spirit is
the opposite of material.

A religious man:
Deals with material: houses of worship, books, talismans, ceremonies, religious artifacts, and clothing.

A spiritual man:
Does not deal with religion or material, but communicates with God / *The Creation* without any additional accessories, but with modesty and inner quiet.

"There are no religions in the universe, but faith".

• **The humankind on Earth was created by *The Creators*,** which are the extraterrestrial aliens, while planet Earth serves as an experimental lab to all life forms.

Jesus (Joshua) was sent by *The Creation* to Earth to undo the religions and open a new Age without religions and material slavery, but absurdly and unintentionally Christianity was founded in his name.

What's absurd is: the establishment of the 'state' of the Vatican in Rome under the Pope, when it's known that the Romans crucified and killed Jesus. Therefore, a biblical karma will destroy all organizations which are based on corrupted foundations.

The three main religions: Christianity, Judaism, and Islam expanded and were blown out of proportion, using extreme controls, threats, and intimidations by:

• Dictating to their followers that they must arrive to prayer complexes and religious classes, setting dates of holidays and ceremonies, asserting what and when to eat, determining on which days to strike and fast, receiving donations up to the establishment of cults or radical factions, prohibiting the mix between believers from different religions; especially when it comes to marriage or burial, then it gets even more absurd:

▪ Declaring that marriage ceremonies may only unite those who believe in the same religion.

▪ Mandating that in burial ceremonies, only 'their believers' be allowed to be buried on 'their land'.

● **All religions work in the form of unnecessary mediation agencies** between humans and *The Creation* (God), while they have been funded by governments, the public, and generations of believers.
You do not need any mediators to reach God. You are associated with *The Creation* by your very creation.

● **Between all religions there is a consistent marketing competition** that promises to unite their believers, assures to bring them 'closer to God', and transform them to 'better people' by giving them answers from the 'holy' books, written by men from ancient times, in their language and point of view, which mostly contain tales from the old days.

● **Material will never be holy, except for the spirit.**
Religion is not spirituality but revolves around the matter and it's contrary to human freedom.

● **The industrial-religion is and has been rolling tons of money** for generations by the exploitation and servitude of their believers into slaves in 'the name of God', by combining brainwashing and fear, without innovation.

• **Human beings have an ego; therefore, religions will not be able to exist in peace.** Historical evidence reflects religions have never united, but divided and dispersed hatred up to the extinction of all that is different, and unfortunately, it still happens nowadays.

*Religion goes against human freedom of choice. In the universe, there is **no religion – but only faith.** It is the inner faith that makes the difference and not the external appearance. **In every aspect of life, the moment you ask 'why' and do not receive a logical answer, it is time to rethink the matter.***

"Around the world people pay their respects to glorify religious leaders clothed in various outfits.

Who is portrayed as more reliable and trustworthy than true people of the spirit, such as mystics and mediums who are portrayed as flighty, strange, or charlatans?

Person's outward appearance and clothing do not indicate his quality, integrity, reliability and true personality."

As the level of education increases, religion will decline. Every new creation - requires chaos first!

• **Chaos =** Destruction for the purpose of a better new creation, as explained below:

- In order to renovate, to create order at home or anywhere, you must create chaos, i.e., make a mess and cleanup, arrange and organize until the desired order is created.

- Creation of a planet requires chaos and the explosion of other planets, after which a new planet will be created from their stardust.

- After the chaos of the Holocaust, the Jewish people were given the right to return from exile and establish a state in the Land of Israel, otherwise it would have never existed.

- In order to wipe-out the religions, chaos must be created, as every new creation requires the destruction of the former.

The purpose of the universe:

You were created by the extraterrestrials / *The Creators* on Earth (which is used as a laboratory for experiments) for the purpose of creating human beings, and you (which were created) will create other human beings and so on, endlessly. Everything around you contains a soul; you are a ball of light embodied in a temporary body of matter.

The purpose of the spirit: to attest to its real nature and by that to testify to the nature of *The Creation* / God.

The purpose of the material: to continue the engine of *The Creation* through a technological-scientific-spiritual creation which progresses infinitely.

Here are some insights:

• **Do not take anything for granted.** There can't be a single truth. Continue to explore infinitely.

The Creation will never provide one final answer but will hide themselves and the answers, in order to allow a choice, to discover. If all was known, then there would be no point in the continuity of life. A mystery is permanent, this is the infinite motor of humanity.

• **The abundance is stabilizing and the lack is motivating.** It's adapted to all areas of life.

• **The number of souls in the universe is limited.** Every soul that comes in, requires another soul to leave and every birth requires the death of another.
The Creation will always allow humanity the **freedom of choice** and if humanity approaches self-destruction, then *The Creation* will intervene to prevent it, as is happening today.

• **Humans will not be able to destroy Earth, but only the temporary life on it.** The Earth lives billions of years and it does not need oxygen, water, soil, or natural resources to survive, yet humans, animals, and nature do need them.

• **You were created** on Earth by the extraterrestrials / *The Creators*, in order to create human life, animals and nature, in order to attest to the nature of the spirit which is embodied in the matter.

• **The material cannot please the soul** for long, emotions are associated with the soul and not with the matter.

• **It is not possible to heal a soul by means of material alone;** each person has the natural capability to heal his own soul and body.

• **Everything lives and breathes around you** with resonance and frequency, on Earth where everything is connected and dependent on one another.

All around you is linked; the movement of one affects all the rest. So, destruction in one part of Earth, affects all parts. Continued environmental destruction in one part, will cause natural disasters in other parts.

On Earth, **states of matter** can be changed, but never annihilated or destroyed.

• **You are infinite balls of light who choose to be embodied in a temporary body on Earth,** in order to testify to the nature of your spirit to *The Creation.*

• **You cannot die.**
Life has no beginning and no end.

The Material world

You choose to be embodied in the following hierarchy of matter:

- ✓ Dust, stone.
- ✓ Plant.
- ✓ Animal.
- ✓ Human beings or form of extraterrestrial.
- ✓ Up to enlightenment in the living body.

The Spirit World

You will end your incarnations in a material world, according to the amount of enlightenment within you as a spirit, and you will be able to rise above as:

- ✓ Entity.
- ✓ Angel.
- ✓ Return to its original state as light and unite with *The Creation*.

At the time of death, you return your soul to the bank of souls and go back to the original state as *a ball of light* and choose without ego to reincarnate again. You can return thousands of incarnations, to the point where you reach enlightenment in a physical body.

You choose to reincarnate in a body such as: dust, dirt, stone, plant, animal, human being, alien, light being, angel, etc. until it returns to its original source as light.

The amount of enlightenment within you is what enables you to rise from the material world, to its place in the hierarchy of the spiritual world.

The universe is in the dark and there are only a few bright spots, the sun shines half a day to allow humanity to discover what already exists in darkness.

After death, *The Creation* will never be angry or punish you, but will give compassion and love to all. You can move up the spiritual hierarchy or go back to the physical hierarchy to correct your way.

About me

As a child, my parents were busy providing and I had a great deal of quality time by myself with an active imagination, patience with fearlessness of experiencing new things. At the age of six, I began to hear and see beyond and had conversations with deceased relatives. I noticed that when I asked a question - then a reply immediately popped into my mind with a vision. At the time, I thought that my experiences were typical to all children, but over the years I discovered that <u>I'm the weird one who is the exception.</u> Out of boredom and loneliness, I opened up to the world of the spirit, there I felt protected and there was no one to stop me or doubt my inner world.

Over the years, I completed my studies in architectural engineering and worked for many years in this field, yet I received a message that my real destiny is to transfer messages, especially while humanity is entering the Aquarius Age during my lifetime. As the years went by, I found out with the help of hypnosis that **I came from the future, from the year 3126, which is the middle of the Aquarius Age.** (More about this age in my The Aquarius Age book.)

I'm a spiritual woman, non-religious but full of endless faith in *The Creation* and *The Creators* because religion contradicts the human freedom of choice. I serve as a vessel for passing through messages and information.

Mystical events in my life

Realization of destiny

*D*uring my twenties, after many years of working as a practical architecture engineer, I decided to quit my job after receiving an inner message: *"My dear, it is time for you to go. The department is about to close down. This is the right time for you **to begin fulfilling your true destiny.**"* I shared this message with my manager, but despite his lack of faith a short time after I left, my prediction came true! This incident strengthened my sense of confidence to fulfill my destiny, working as a medium.

A messenger

I entered a restaurant and noticed an old man in tattered clothes looking-through the restaurant's window, it felt as if only I saw him. I went outside and put some money in his hand; he returned it back and said: *"I don't want your money; I want to eat."* He refused to come inside and stayed on the sidewalk. I bought him a meal and gave it to him. He kissed my palm and took it. On my way back inside, I turned back to him but he vanished! He was a messenger who was sent to test me.

Encounter with extraterrestrials (aliens)

*O*ne night I woke up and felt my entire body paralyzed except the blinking of my eyes. I saw two aliens standing in front of me, looking at me, their appearance was:

a bit taller than a typical human, head shaped like an upturned pear, eyes large and cat-like, no eyelashes or body hair, small mouths, and noses. I wasn't afraid and began to communicate with them through telepathy: *"Why did it take you so long to come? I've been waiting for you since an early age."* They responded: *"We've been here all the time; **you are the one** who wasn't ready"*.

I remembered from that encounter how my body rose in the air and with a single blink they rotated me as I was floating in the air, so that I faced the floor and were led through my room's open window to a round spaceship covered with small illuminated windows with unusual structure of chains that made up the spaceship's floor. I received some kind of treatment in the spaceship, but they erased my memory afterwards. In that same night, I received the ability of x-ray vision, even remotely. In the following day, I woke up extremely tired. Over the years up to these days, I continue to communicate with them.

Trip to London

I went with a friend to London. We took a ferry at the River Thames. During that cruise, I closed my eyes and saw a vision: 'the entire city of London is on fire'. A few weeks later, I learned of *'The Great Fire of London'* that broke out in the year 1666! As we were celebrating my birthday, we went into a big toy store on Oxford Street. My friend announced to one of the salesmen that I'm a medium, to which he insisted to receive a personal message, so I told him: *"You were here in London at the age of 17 on a family trip with your parents and your little sister"*, he was stunned and said: *"It's true! How did you know that? I will gather the rest of the employees, please come to the fifth floor."*

Without requesting it, I found myself on the fifth-floor channeling voluntarily to the store's employees. In one special case, one manager approached me, so I asked him: *"Why are you sad? Your sister is already feeling better after her operation."* He was surprised and told me that his sister had undergone heart surgery. I began to see her heart from afar, using 'x-ray vision': *"The source of your sister's heart condition was the lower left valve, which separates the chambers of the heart, it did not function properly and the problem was fixed"*. Immediately, he called his mother who verified all the details were true!

After four hours we came out of the store and while we were standing on Oxford Street, I told my friend to look up at the sky: *"The Creation is sending us a message and a hug from above."* Shortly after, an airplane emerged and marked a white stripe in the sky.

The woman in black

One morning, a 70 years old woman came for a channeling session. She wore a black dress; her hair was black and disheveled. She sat in front of me and began to complain how mystics have 'ruined' her life by not allowing her to ever experience love or marriage.

I felt her negative energy and noticed a satanic male entity dwells within her, so I immediately protected myself and asked the entity within her: *"What have you come to me seeking? What is it that you want? I am protected, you cannot harm me."*

The woman continued complaining and began to curse, so I asked her to leave without paying. An hour later I smelled something burning in the room and when I lifted my head up, I saw a 'fiery flame' erupting from the top of my head. I put out the fire; some burnt pieces of paper fell down but amazingly my hair and scalp weren't damaged. I immediately gathered the energy she sent me as a ball of fire and sent it back to her and I asked from *The Creation* to let justice be done.

Out of body experience

One night, I woke up from my sleep paralyzed without the ability to move, besides my eyes. On the wall in front of me, I saw a wide camera film open up and in it three picture frames. Paralyzed I saw myself in a form of a hovering white dove, flying between several images from my previous incarnations. My soul rose out of my chest and entered into the first picture frame. This process repeated itself three times.

In each frame I saw myself in different places, speaking a different language until the whole process ended. Moments later, a spiral white light appeared in front of me and it began to turn in a circle, while tiny chubby colorful angels, without any gender, were flying around the spiral and heavenly music of harp was in the background. Wow! That was a divine experience!

The prince of darkness / devil

I borrowed a spiritual book, read the first half, and agreed with almost everything written in it. In the following day, while reading the second half, I realized that the contents were not as 'enlightened' as I had thought. I saw it as a moral obligation to note this in my first book, Divine Creation.

At midnight I placed the book on the nightstand and sunk into a deep sleep. Suddenly, I opened my eyes and couldn't move, aside from blinking, I lay on my side paralyzed and felt someone kneeling on my bed behind my back, pressure had been created in the mattress. Someone's elbow pressed into my right arm and I felt pain.

I saw that it was a male figure with a bull's head with thick glowing gold horns, which emerged from the upper part of his forehead. The pain in my right arm gradually intensified. I decided to speak with him voicelessly and politely asked him to leave and not bother me. I heard devious laughter from his throat. I summoned angels and entities to come and help me.

He applied force on my right arm, approached my right ear and whispered: *"Who do you think you are to dare write about me in your book, which will be published world-*

wide? You mustn't write what you've intended to nor slander my name. You are unaware of the fact that I have a respectable position in the universe in order to allow free choice to all. You shall never publish the name of the book you've read and if you do so - then I will visit you again... And while I'm here let's testify your force."

He applied increased force on my right arm and that was so painful. Suddenly, I felt a 'ball of light and fire' stirring in my belly and it reached my chest, entered my right arm which lifted up and pushed him away, he disappeared in an instant. I decided to share that encounter: **the devil does exist and has a place in the universe.**

I realized that good and evil do not exist. Maybe what's good for one person - is bad for the other. Everything is relative.

Everything exists around you in pairs:
Male and female; day and night;
darkness and light;
devil and angels; heaven and hell.
You even have been given the ability to lie,
because always telling the truth
will not enable you to choose.
All is done in order to balance
and allow you with free choice.

My mother's death

Six months before my mother's death, while she was still clear-minded, I had a dream in which my mother appeared alone in a room and told me:

"Hush.... don't tell anyone that I'm here. <u>Only you can see me</u>. They are asking me in Heaven to decide whether to stay here or to leave. What do you suggest I should decide?" I replied: *"Mother, I have no right to decide for you, that is a decision only you can make."* She replied back: *"O.K, I'll think what to do."* After that, I saw the number five.

Friday at four o'clock in the afternoon, I received a message to rush to the hospital. As I began driving toward the hospital, I felt that my mother was sitting in the passenger seat beside me. She said:

"I came to say goodbye. I chose to leave now, on a Friday afternoon when there is little traffic on the roads, because I know how much you hate traffic jams".

As I entered her room in the hospital at five o'clock, (as in my dream!) I found out that my mom passed away while I was driving. In the hospital room, I saw a vision in which she was standing, smiling, healthy, happy and suffering no pain while she entered *'The tunnel of light'*.

We are all made of spirits; therefore, we cannot die, but only change form and keep on moving.

The spirit is infinite. *At each birth you rent a soul from the bank of souls and enter a host body, at the time of birth and exit it, at the time of death. Each event that occurred in your lives **was meant to be - because you chose it!** This is all to achieve personal empowerment, become mature, complete cycles, and make a correction with your karma. You have received the most precious thing, which no one else can give you and that is **life, the only sacred thing.***

You cannot die.
You are infinite balls of light
that testify themselves to The Creation / God,
by learning through being in
a temporary material body, where
all human actions testify to the nature of God.

Fear results from - the lack of knowledge.
Knowledge is power - which chases away fear.
If you know - then there is nothing to fear.

"Once there was a young girl that was a bit odd,
a little shy but with a heart of gold.
She wanted to help those around her
so they would see, how much kindness God gave her.
She asked to feel like she belonged somewhere,
to experience care and love with one another.

She had no books or toys on her shelf,

so she imagined another life and created lots of games
from cardboard and colored pencils, for herself.

When she had no doll to hold,
she made one from a sock that was old.
She played hide and seek by herself and didn't think it was
odd to always have conversations with God.

She spent her childhood in the backyard of an old house,
many years ago, in a distressed neighborhood.

She was blessed with the ability to receive and correspond
with entities that gave her messages,
from the hidden worlds beyond,
which in time were revealed to be true.

And so, she helped other people and her reputation grew.

Channeling gave her happiness, satisfaction, and friends.
She didn't have much fortune - but a heart of gold,
*which was provided to her - by Almighty **God**."*

Chapter 1:
Who are we and where do we come from?

How did humanity first settle on planet Earth? Is man really a descendant of the gorilla or not? What are the Ten Commandments and were there more or less than ten?

As a great believer in *The Creation* (God), I respect religions, but I'm not religious thanks to the freedom of choice. I came from the future, from the middle of the Aquarius age.

I do not belong to any organization, political party, movement or sect. I have no desire or motivation to become a guru or to glorify one person or another, certainly not myself.

All religions contradict the human beings' right to freedom of choice. The moment a religious person dictates to others a list of do's and don'ts which they must follow, he deprives them of their freedom of choice.

A few insights:

• **If there was only one single truth,** then you wouldn't have had the freedom to choose and believe differently, in order to continuously recreate everything in life endlessly.

• In order to reach a decision in life, you should **always listen to both sides,** as a judge does, which is why we have two ears.

• Over the years, **mostly men ruled the world** with the Divide and Conquer strategy. Therefore, men created numerous religions, faiths, languages, educational methods, organizations, stock exchanges, monetary currencies, governments, cities, and so on.

• It is very important that the inhabitants of planet Earth adopt **English as a single world-wide language**, as it is nowadays, where English is used to communicate internationally.

• **Using English as a single language** will help to communicate and will unify all of Earth's inhabitants. Today English is the universal language. It's time to let go of stubbornness and ego regarding whether 'your or my language is ancient or better'. However, every nation has the right to learn and preserve its own ancient language.

• **Humanity must continually make progress,** without being stuck in the past history.

It is unnecessary to preserve the history,
since humanity never learned the
lessons of the past and still repeats the
same mistakes over and over again.

Did the wars of the past teach us to strive for peace?
Or have we only learned to improve the technologies of the
weapons and the methods of spying and destruction?

It is surprising that most of the religion books display continuity, the unified chronological sequence of events, spanning thousands of years and 'miraculously' gathered it all into a single book. How is this possible?

• **Religious and history books,** like all books, are written from the personal point of view of their authors; **they only represent their personal 'truth'.** As you know, there are two sides to every coin, which is why you must always hear the other side's opinion, to understand the complete truth.

Remember: The other side will always have its own 'truth', which is different from yours, but still, it's the same story with two sides of view.

God, The Creators, and The Created

God / *The Creation*

The meaning of God or the Creation's Entities is to constantly replicate themselves and recreate the universe at every moment.

God created **The Creators,**
so they could create **The Created.**

On Earth each life form creates other life forms.

God / *The Creation* is an infinite cosmic energy, full of light and love. **It creates** endless worlds, stars, planets, darkness, lights, and souls, while it duplicates itself nonstop.

The Creators

• *The Creators* are responsible for creating various humanity and other life forms on planet Earth.
• *The Creators* **cannot create** universes, stars, darkness, lights, and souls. Only God / *The Creation* can.
• *The Creators* are specific kind of extraterrestrial / *aliens* from, which exist on Earth as many different life forms.
• *The Creators* must adhere to the universe law: freedom of choice for all. Therefore, they must allow any living form to have freedom of choice (rule No. 1). But they supervise what

happens on planet Earth and try not to interfere. Only when things get out of control, then *The Creators* offer assistance in order to prevent mankind from annihilating themselves.

Planet Earth is used as an experimental laboratory of The Creators, with the aid of advanced technologies from their planets.

The Creators have created
The Created: the mankind,
By hybridizing a male gorilla with an alien female.

The Created

The Creators created **all of Earth's mankind with free will, which are called *The Created,*** by hybridizing a male gorilla with an alien female.

The mission of humanity and all life forms around the universe is to endlessly create. This is the engine of *The Creation.*

God / *The Creation*

A cosmic energy, which created the universe
and infinitely duplicates itself.

The Creators

Are certain kind of extra-terrestrial / aliens,
which created all mankind on Earth.

The Created

Are all of Earth's mankind, who are also designed to create
advanced human beings, which will create another advanced
human beings on other planets, and so on in an infinite loop
of creation.

In the beginning, God created

The entire universe exists in the darkness. God / *The Creation* wanted to create dynamics in the darkness and therefore, decided to create life forms, planets, and stars which introduced some light into the darkness.

"And God saw the light, that it was good":
These words testify to the fact that God / *The Creation* created the universe through a process of trial and error: creating, operating, changing, upgrading, and correcting.

1 "In the beginning, God created the heaven and the earth.

2 And the earth was without form and void, and darkness was upon the face of the deep. And the Spirit of God moved upon the face of the waters.

3 And God said, let there be light: and there was light.

4 And God saw the light, that it was good: and God divided the light from the darkness.

5 And God called the light Day, and the darkness Night. And the evening and the morning were the first days.

16 And God made two great lights; the greater light to rule the day, and the lesser light to rule the night; he made the stars also.

17 And God set them in the firmament of the heaven to give light upon the earth.

18 And to rule over the day and over the night, and to divide the light from the darkness; and God saw that it was good".

Verse Number 1:

1 "God created the heaven"
The infinite space, where one cannot naturally walk in the physical dimension, but in the spiritual dimension as a spirit.

"And the earth"
God / *The Creation* created planet Earth within infinite space; the Earth is where one can naturally walk in the physical dimension.

"And the earth was without form and void"
At the beginning, God / *The Creation* chose to create spirits and planets. In order to do so, **you must create chaos first.**

"God made the stars also"
Each galaxy contains a number of **planets that emit light in the great darkness:** the Moon (which illuminates during the night) and the Sun (which illuminates during the day).

Verse Number 2

2 "And the earth was without form and void, and darkness was upon the face of the deep. And the Spirit of God moved upon the face of the waters."

"And the earth was without form and void"
Planet Earth was created at the beginning from **chaos without form.**

"And darkness was upon the face of the deep"
The universe is **a bottomless vacuum without boundaries,** which also exists in the darkness that surrounds the Earth.

"And the Spirit of God moved upon the face of the waters"
God / *The Creation* is made up of spirts that **received life through the water and breathed life into a living body.** Where there is water - there is life.

Verse Number 3

3 "And God said, let there be light: and there was light"
God / *The Creation* 'said' let there be light and light was created.

Everything that you say or think - it's all energy that **you create and returns to you.**

Everything exists in the present, in layers upon layers, so there is no past-present-future in the structure of time. There is no time, only light and darkness.

It is only a movement between darkness and light.
You will notice the arrival of the evening, when the sun sets.
When you fall asleep, you move from light to darkness.
Babies arrive from darkness inside the mother's womb, into light.
Once you close your eyes, at the moment of death, you move from light to darkness.
Only in the darkness you are able to notice the light.

Humanity invented the time, in order to define the movement of life on Earth.

Verse Number 4

4 "And God saw the light, that it was good"
God / *The Creation* created the light, using the trial-and-error method and saw that it was good and beneficial.
Darkness is the natural state of the universe; therefore, it was created first and then light.

Everything exists in the darkness and light helps to reveal what already exists in the darkness.

You were created from darkness and to darkness you shall return. The light is temporary and the darkness is permanent.

Accept the darkness as a background color upon which you can shine your internal light.

Darkness should not be feared. People give it mistaken connotations of evil and the unknown. Light is temporary, local, and emitted from stars. **Darkness is the natural state.**

All creation of life occurs in the dark, such as the birth and death of all living forms or stars.

Verse Number 5

5 *"And God called the light Day, and the darkness Night. And the evening and the morning were the first days".*
God / *The Creation* allowed both light and darkness to exist at their proper times. The light during the day and the darkness during the night. It allows order and rest for humanity, with night and morning making up a single day.

Verses 16 – 18

16 *"And God made two great lights; the greater light to rule the day, and the lesser light to rule the night; he made the stars also".*

17 *And God set them in the firmament of the heaven to give light upon the earth,*

18 *And to rule over the day and over the night, and to divide the light from the darkness; and God saw that it was good".*

"And God saw that it was good".

This is the continuation of the **trial-and-error experiment,** an experiment that succeeded - *"God saw that it turned out well".*

God / *The Creation* decided to **illuminate the darkness of the universe** with some local celestial flashlights (just like street lights illuminate large areas).

In the realm of the lesser light, the Moon illuminates during the short night, and in the realm of the greater light, the Sun illuminates during the long day.

The daytime is much longer than the nighttime in order to allow mankind **to discover throughout the day, that which exists in darkness.**

The settlement on planet Earth

In order to create, chaos must first be produced.

As you renovate a house, at first there is a lot of mess and disorder, and once things are put in order, repaired, or replaced, then a new creation is achieved.

A brief explanation of *The Creation* process:

While stars and planets explode against one another, only then they are able to duplicate themselves. Yet, spirits can only be exchanged among themselves.

In order for a spirit to enter a human body at birth, another must leave a body at the time of death, because there must be exchanges between a fixed number of spirits.

First, God / *The Creation* created the water, the foundation for the existence of life. It was done by sending enormous meteors of ice to Earth. That's how oceans and seas were created.

Second, volcanoes were created as nature developed and life forms took shape on planet Earth. Then *The Creators* (aliens) arrived and created a new human breed.

Life on Earth began billions of years ago with
*a **'leasing' agreement** between*
***God / The Creation** and The Creators,*
to create a new human breed
by the hybridization between
a male gorilla and a female alien.

Boundaries

Human beings find it difficult to accept the fact they live in a boundless world.

This difficulty results from the 'fear of the unknown' that causes human beings to divide and conquer, to establish laws and create rules, in order to produce their own 'order':

• Boundaries in time and date.
• Boundaries at sea, land, and the air.
• Boundaries between countries, territories, etc.

The world is boundless and so are the Earth and the sea. Open a window and you will see that nature does not exist in straight lines and all lines are crooked and connect together. In this period, life on Earth is restrictive and doesn't allow for personal freedom.

Here are a few explanations:

• Luckily enough, the air on Earth is boundless and limitless. It is everywhere and crosses into space.

• The continents and oceans on Earth are more than we have been told, were created without any boundaries and limitations, and were given to all mankind equally regardless of religion, race, gender, or nationality.

• The moment a man's movement on Earth is limited; his freedom of choice (rule 1) is denied. This negative energy returns in a cyclical movement (rule 2) and creates wars among human beings, as is explained in Chapter 3.

Because of **the lack of freedom,** as a result of deep awareness and excessive use of 'force of law' beyond the boundaries of reason, this is a necessary chaos for citizens to demonstrate, rebel, and fight against governments and regimes.

Human beings, out of ego and existential fear, have conquered lands by force, declared them to be their own, separated themselves from others with borders on sea and land, and have given themselves their own identifying marks, such as flag, nationality, religion, language, and culture. Humanity cannot see the complete picture, which is that human beings may be different from one another in their appearance, language and opinions, but they all possess a spirit, which is common to all of mankind.

Everyone was created naked and possessed freedom of choice and had the right to live, work, study, learn, travel, eat, dress, be born, buried, or cremated, wherever they choose in any country, regardless of borders and government permission.

As we are entering the Aquarius Age, that will officially start from the year 2106, there will be world-wide communities, without governments nor boundaries, world peace from 2025 on going, as I wrote in my other books.

Human beings will not own materials, everything will be shared. The only thing humanity owns is not their fortune or soul, **but only their freedom of choice.**

Noah's Ark

Once the Earth was endowed only with the elements of nature, *The Creators* decided to populate the planet with animals on the sea and on land. They conducted many experiments on their planet and created many types of animals, male and female for breeding purposes, and brought them to planet Earth in **Noah's Ark,** which was their spacecraft.

• Over billions of years, *The Creators* had **performed many experiments** on their animals on Earth. Over time, the growth of the animals went out of control and they reached enormous dimensions, then *The Creators* / aliens decided to end that era and to start anew. They collected to a spacecraft (Noah's ark) many animal species, male and female for future breeding.

• **In order to create again, first there must be a chaos.** This was produced by the **flood** of enormous **meteors made of ice** and originated from the outer space. Even after the meteors were burnt in the Earth's atmosphere, they remained large enough to destroy life on Earth, but not the planet itself.

• Then Earth underwent cataclysmic change, which started the **Ice Age.** Eventually, the Earth thawed and returned to a state that would allow the existence of life again.

• Once the Earth could be inhabited again, *The Creators / aliens* **returned to Earth** in a spacecraft / Noah's Ark with many animal species (male and female) which were collected before the flood and **upgraded since then.**

• Based on past experience, *The Creators* decided to populate the Earth not only with animals, but also with human beings who they created in a **crossbreeding process between male animal gorilla and female alien.**

God / The Creation created man in his own image. All spirits were created from a divine spark of God's spirit and will exist forever.

The Created are all living forms and humanity on planet Earth, which were created by The Creators, which are the aliens, while the formula is: one race creates another.

The creation of mankind

The Creators /aliens created *The Created,* which are three species of human beings on Earth, using crossbreeding of a male gorilla with a female alien.

• The Japanese were created first. They are the most ancient species. Japan is the country that invented and refined global technology from the 1970's to the present, with companies such as:
Sony, Toshiba, Teac, JVC, Akai, Sharp, Fujitsu, Panasonic, Pioneer, Nikon, Yamaha, Casio, Mitsubishi, etc. (in general, the Chinese are experts at copying, but not creating).

• Creation of man began thousands of years ago in Japan, they are the most similar to *Our Creators* / the aliens, and from there, humanity spread globally through Asia.

• Throughout the world, there are countless human species, each with its own form, look and features. While we are known by the name 'human beings', the other forms of life / aliens are also human and have a destiny of creating a new human race, in order to testify to the nature of God / *The Creation*.

The origin of the Human Race

Our Creators are aliens from distant planets and they created three species of human beings on Earth.

The first was the Japanese one, which was created similarly to our alien Creators' appearance:

• Skinny bodies with long hands that reach their knees.
• A small mouth, large and slanted eyes with dark pupils, without eyelashes or body hair.
• Bumps on their faces that serve as nostrils, without an external nose bone.

Our alien *Creators* communicate mainly through telepathy and by writing symbols with emotionless robotic thinking.

Similarities of Japanese to the aliens:

A higher percentage of DNA from our alien *Creators*, than the male gorilla.

Short, straight black hair; small and flattened nose.

Slanted eyes, skinny, short, and their body is hairless.

The Japanese also have a lot of rituals and code of conduct of their own, extreme devotion working around the clock, act like robots with inhumane standards, show little emotion, and their written language is made of symbols.

Over time, two additional human species were created by *The Creators* based on the different climatic conditions on continents.
By mating with each other, these three basic human species created a large variety of human appearances, as they exist

today. Over the years, the climate, food and area of habitation influenced the skin tone, hair, and eyes of all three species, based on the exposure to sunlight, and the different levels of vitamin D.

The Creators created three human species separate from each other:

The Asian Human Specie - has a higher percentage of female alien DNA and a lower percentage of male gorilla DNA. This is how human beings were created, which are **similar in their appearance to aliens.**

Male Gorilla	Female Alien

The Dark-Skinned Specie - has a higher percentage of male gorilla DNA and a lower percentage of female alien DNA. This is how human beings were created, which are **similar in their appearance to gorillas.**

Male Gorilla	Female Alien

The Varied-Skinned Specie - has the same percentage between the female alien DNA and the male gorilla DNA. This is how human beings were created, which are **similar in their appearance to the average between the gorilla and alien.**

Male Gorilla	Female Alien

Created first: Asian man	Created second: Dark-skinned man	Created third: Varied-skinned man
DNA Crossbreeding with a **high percentage of female alien DNA** and **low percentage of gorilla DNA**	DNA Crossbreeding with a **low percentage of female alien DNA** and **high percentage of gorilla DNA.**	DNA Crossbreeding with **similar percentage of female alien DNA** and **gorilla DNA.**
Similarities to aliens: Light skin tone. Slanted eyes, skinny and short, straight hair, no body hair. Symbolic writing language, robotic thinking. Areas of habitat: Moderate climate. **Asia.**	Similarities to gorillas: Dark skin tone. Dark hair and eyes. Thick curly hair. Flattened nose, muscular, possess a high level of physical power and testosterone. Areas of habitat: Warm climate. **Africa.**	Similarities: Variety of: Skin tone, height, eye color, hair types such as straight, wavy light, and curly. Areas of habitat: Cold climate. **Europe, America.**

The origin of Man and Woman

Woman	Man
The origin of **woman** is from **the alien**.	The origin of **man** is from the **gorilla**.
Similarities to alien -Narrow, small, low body mass, small skull. -Thin physique, narrow waist and refined face. -Lower physical power and high level of spiritual and telepathic strength. -As gatherer can perform multiple tasks at the same time, as a computer. -Delicate, well-groomed, caring, maternal, less ego, and more peace-loving. -More sentimental for the needs of others. -Occupations that require integrated action, responsibility, help, tolerance and to educate.	**Similarities to gorilla** -Large body mass, wide and tall, large skull. -Muscular upper body part and legs. -Possesses a high level of physical power and testosterone. -Hunters who can perform one activity each time. -Aggressive, warriors, with egos and an inclination to rule as the head of the tribe. -Less sentimental, and more logical mind. -Occupations that require physical strength and logical thinking.

The differences between man and woman

• **Woman** originates from **the alien.** She is able to perform multiple tasks like a computer. Such abilities prepared her to become a gatherer who is able to perform several simultaneous tasks.

• **Man** originates from **the gorilla.** He is a hunter who can perform mostly a single task each time. Men are busy with survival; they possess ego and pride, as the gorillas are 'the leaders of the pack'.

• Statistically, women have longer life spans than men.

• In most cases, **women are more spiritual** than men. They possess intuition and a greater openness to receive messages and communications from the world, as the aliens do. Therefore, women are usually involved in the spiritual world.

• **Migraines** most often affect women. Migraines are a spiritual factor which influences the physical body when the channel ability is not expressed in practice.

Migraines are energies that start from the crown chakra (located at the top of the head) and descend to the third eye chakra (located in the forehead between the eyes) and control the temples.

This is the process of receiving messages and communicating with the world. If this information is not channeled outside, then the energy creates a physical pressure on the forehead and temples area.

• **Men** were intended to perform projects that require **great physical strength.** Similar to gorillas, men are strong, sturdy, muscular and have a high level of testosterone which leads to hair growth all over their bodies, including facial hair.

Like gorillas, most men enjoy living in small packs and rule their kingdom like 'the king of the gorillas'.

In the Pisces Age men ruled, that's why humanity began to organize in smaller tribes, villages and small family units. Like the gorillas, the behavior of most men is based on ego and existential fear. As a result, they act violently and aggressively and they tend not to act out of emotion, which they consider unmanly.

• In the last century, childhood vaccines contained high amounts of hormones that caused women and men to change their gender. Vaccines contained ingredients for infertility and diseases, in order to control human health, to enrich pharmaceutical companies, and to create depopulation on behalf of governments which are scared of the masses. All this will disappear with the arrival of the Age of Aquarius.

• **Men find it difficult to share a woman with other men,** because of their totalitarian outlook. A woman can share herself with several men without any physical or moral problems.

• **Women are generally more refined than men.**
As opposed to men, women are able to live in bigger tribes
or large groups based on their desire for personal freedom.
Women can share one husband with other women (just like
the kings and rulers of the past who had several wives).

• **Women are aliens,** therefore are **bi-sexual.** It is common
to see women of every age holding each other's hands or
kissing. Women are much more open-minded, both sexually
and mentally, and their emotional side is dominant. Women
can share their love with others, both males and females,
without any difficulty.

• **Most men are heterosexual** who tend to recoil from
touching other men. Most of them are jealous and demand
that their women remain with them throughout their lives,
while women seek out new loves and thrills in their lives.
That is why there are tensions between the sexes.

The human soul is what pushes a person to be unfaithful. It's
simply the basic need of a human being to reach for love as
love is the fuel of the soul, otherwise, without love you might
become ill.

Remember the first rule: The only thing that you own is
your freedom of choice and it should not be touched.

It is the right of any person to experience love, without
being forced to act in a way that contradicts the will of his
soul.

• **The women bring balance** that counteracts the men's destructive powers. Men mostly act out of emotionless common sense, ego, and existential fear. If not for women, men would bring about the destruction and annihilation of humanity on Earth. The pages of history are filled with stories of wars and conflicts, which were planned and executed by men.

• **The role of women on Earth is to balance the wild and animalistic power of men.** They are strong, dominate, and the 'leaders of the pack'. That's why during the Pisces Age, the vast majority of world leaders were men.

• The source of life is within the female, which can create life, therefore **females are the cosmic alien factory.**

Everything exists forever

Every tree that is uprooted and every fruit that is plucked, will grow again.

Every forest that is destroyed by fire or a polluted ocean, will recover. Everything is perpetually renewed!

If we look at a piece of material, such as, wood, cloth, glass, plastic or metal, under a microscope, we will discover that the atoms are constantly moving, because **everything exists forever, in each and every state of matter and form!**

Nothing can go extinct or be killed. Even in death, the soul leaves the body which is perishable, returned to the bank of souls, and then as a spirit you go back to your state as ball of light and can return again and rent a soul in order to inhabit a different body, if you choose so.

Nature is everything that grows, air, water, human beings, and animals, from germs and up to mankind.

Everything contains energies and frequencies which breathe, multiply, expand, and contract.

Without nature, there is no life!

You cannot destroy or stop anything in nature.

Everything lives and exists forever.

Nature, air and light

Air and light are full of an energy, called 'Prahna', which means a *force of life, breath, soul, or cosmic power*. It is the **vibration that exists** in everything. 'Prahna' connects the organs of the physical body with the circulatory systems, which lead to the heart.

'Prahna' connects the soul to the spiritual body through chakras and auras, which are connected by dots and lead to the soul. While looking at air or water in daylight, **one can see the 'Prahna' as rounded shapes, transparent spheres,** often with a center dot in various colors, which can often be captured with a camera.
Music and scents also have colors and shapes of their own, which can be perceived through the ten senses.

Air, light, earth, water, and music are all part of *The Creation's* vibrations and such vibrations influence the emotional and energetic bodies.

Preserving planet Earth

Essentially, you are a ball of light, spirit, which inhabits a physical body with a rented soul for a short time on Earth. As a spirit, you can change identities and bodies in each incarnation.

The physical body has no life without the temporary soul.

Human beings have an egotistical way of thinking, as if everything is permitted since 'we own it all'. This type of egotistical viewpoint could bring to the destruction of nature and the environment, as nowadays most of the land and water resources are polluted and animals are slaughtered excessively on land and in the sea.

*"Whales and dolphins must not be killed. These are ancient animals that conceal within them the 'secret of The Creation'. These are not the ones in danger of extinction - **human beings are!**"*

"You are all guests for a short stay on the face of the Earth. You are all spirits whose souls have been lent to you in each incarnation. You choose a host body and breathe life into it, you don't possess any matter in the world, other than your own freedom of choice".

The elderly and the ancient

"Stand up in the presence of the aged and show respect for the elderly and what is ancient".

This verse, calls on us not only to revere the elderly, but also to revere nature, which is ancient and existed before human beings were created.

All of mankind's actions come back to him (Rule No. 2), so therefore, the moment humanity destroys the resources of nature, future generations will no longer possess the basis for life and they will gradually become extinct.

The moment mankind goes too far, *The Creators* will create and send chaos to Earth, such as a 'fake pandemic' in order to reveal the hidden truth, depopulate corrupted people and those who choose material over spirituality along with faith in God, and were blindly obeying without further investigation. However, the foundations of Earth will not be destroyed.

Tips for life

• Work, study, eat, and drink moderately. Protect the freedom.

• Don't believe yet always research.

• Learn to touch and demonstrate love, show tolerance and care for one another. **Love in its lower frequency reveals itself through sex and in its higher frequency through compassion.**

• Expand your horizons, travel, and enjoy nature.

• Get to know your neighbors across the globe, with respect and tolerance.

The memories and insights
you gather during your lifetime
are the only things you will take with you
to your next incarnation.

At the moment of death, when you reach 'The Heavens', then you will be asked the following by *The Creation:*

 "What have you done to benefit yourself, others, and the environment? What mission have you accomplished?"

In other words, you will be asked the following:
Have **you** experienced love, what have **you** learned, what kind of education and insights have **you** achieved for yourself, what have **you** seen, how have **you** advanced humanity, and how have **you** helped people and the environment with your knowledge?

You would not be asked: *"How many children you had or how much money you earned. These are not the missions of life".*

Chapter 2:
God, religion, and other insights

Who is God / *The Creation*?
Is it a single or plural entity?
What language does he speak?
Why doesn't he reveal himself to us?
There are no religions in the universe, but only faith.

• **God is an infinite cosmic energy full of light, love which duplicates itself constantly, and exists everywhere and in everything.**
It creates worlds, stars, spirits, souls, and all the matters.
It gave human beings freedom of choice, so they could choose. God speaks all languages.

• **It is wrong to ascribe to God human emotions, such as anger, hatred, or 'the wrath of God'.** These are all human concepts.

• **God is not 'an old man' dressed in white and sitting up in the Heavens.** It is gender-free and doesn't have a physical body and often manifests 'itself' via messengers in a physical body on Earth.

• **God is everywhere in spirit and in the matter, which renews itself in a cyclical and endless way.**

• **Nothing is yours except your freedom of choice.** All was given to you by its grace, every book, article, invention, knowledge, or idea originates from God / *The Creation!*

You were created by The Creators, in order to testify to the nature of you and God / The Creation!

How would you know who you are without looking in a mirror of your soul?

Each and every one of your actions testify to the nature of God / The Creation.

How can God / The Creation know whether it is good, merciful, loving, generous, helpful, hateful, or cruel?

Insights about religion

God / *The Creation* did not create religions, but human beings did. There are no religions in the universe, but only FAITH, as:

1. Religions were created by humanity on Earth, in order to prevent the primitive nature of human beings from ruining themselves and their environment.

2. Human beings find it difficult to live without boundaries (although the world has no boundaries), plus the addition of 'The freedom of choice' to people, makes it much more difficult to control humanity.

3. Human beings have sought a 'responsible adult' to take care of them and take them under God's wing, like a child attached to his parents. Human beings seek supervision out of fear of themselves and from the unknown.

4. Human beings will always search for their creator and have found many ways to channel with **God / *The Creation*.** Parts of this communication were documented in the ancient books, the Bible.

5. The initial goal of inventing religion was to connect the material (the human body) and the spiritual with God / *The Creation*, to whom the spirits of all belong.
However, over time religion became more powerful and a way to solve or escape one's troubles. As religion grew stronger the use of force and intimidation increased, often

accompanied by coercion and threats, brainwashing of false promises, and lies.

6. In a place where there is knowledge and people who are investigating, then religious coercion loses its power.

• **God / *The Creation* is made up of a cosmic energetic spirit of love,** which surrounds everything as an endless powerful tornado that renews and duplicates itself at every given moment.

• **The only thing that is sacred is life, spirit, and soul, so start getting used to it.** There are no sacred places, but only ancient places. There are no sacred books, but only ancient books.

• **God / *The Creation* does not reveal his real image to humanity,** because its energy mass is so vast that it could cause spiritual damage to all material creatures.

• **God / *The Creation* did not create religions or temples, which were created by humanity.**
God only wants you to acknowledge his existence and will never ask you to worship him, because he knows his glory. This is in the same way that you don't worship your parents who brought you into the world.

• **God / *The Creation* never asked you for anything material** or to make sacrifices, build prayer houses or worship with daily prayers, to turn your lives into blind worship. It also didn't ask for coffins or tombstones. These originated from the ceremonies of the past.

• *The Creators* **are alien species who created you,** in the same way that other creators created other breeds of humans.

• **God /** *The Creation* **helps those who help themselves.** A man must first show some effort in order to receive help. Prayer has a wonderful power to create, just like imagination. **The moment to imagine, then you create!**

With every thought, saying, and deed, you create your own reality, as an energy coming back to you. There is no problem to gather and pray together as long as it is done out of free choice.
• Remember: being good will bring you goodness in return, and will testify the character of God / *The Creation*.

• **God /** *The Creation* **will not decide or limit you,** and will not interfere with your freedom of choice, but will put a limit once humanity is about to reach self-destruction.

• **Religions deny mankind's freedom of choice.**
Religions dictate holidays and laws for their believers, because the believers are committed to do as they are told. The more extremist and forceful the religions are, the more they remove from free-will and **God /** *The Creation*.

• **Religions and the male ego are the reasons for segregation and war between nations.** As proof, one only needs to leaf through the pages of history.

• **God /** *The Creation* **is full of love.** There are no punishments, nor 'God's Chariots', nor 'God's wrath'. **God will never hate, judge, or punish you.**

• After your death, **God /** *The Creation* **will not punish you, but will give you the chance to judge yourself** and to explain your essence where you went wrong. **You are being loved for eternity.**

• **Everything takes place sequentially and in parallel. There is no past or future, only the present exists.** You are creating a new present in every single moment, layers upon layers. Every action cancels the previous one and creates a new one, that is *The Creation's engine.*

• **The ancient writings (Bible) are, in part, a collection of stories.** Ancient writings and the various books of any Bible were written by various authors who documented over the course of many generations various events in their own words and according to their personal viewpoints. Some of the events did actually take place in reality, while others were invented through legends, folk tales, and stories.

• **The ten commandments are a fraud:** Everything is written as 'requirements from God', as 'you shall not do this or that' in order to control humans.

God / *The Creation* will never dictate you but provides all with free choice.

God will NEVER tell you what to do. The divine simple formula is: What you do, comes back to you, and after death, you judge yourself.

Did you ever stop to think for a moment, what is allowed, if many things are forbidden? Where is the 'you shall do and enjoy?' Where is the choice and the fun? Perhaps someone omitted those commandments on purpose, in order to control population.

Try to picture yourself going on a trip, and from the very beginning, the guide imposes various restrictions and prohibitions. You think to yourselves 'If that's the way the trip begins, I'm definitely not going to have fun'.

In order to reign in the primitive nature of humanity,
men of power with a narrow and strict view of the world,
chose to remove from the ancient writings,
in order to control the freedom of choice.
This is how religions began to control human beings, by
claiming that this is 'what God commanded'.

Since when does God give commands?
Make demands? Give out punishments?

God / *The Creation* will never use force,
but only the spirit of love.

"Neither by might nor by power,
but by my spirit, I am the LORD".

• **God / *The Creation* speaks in all languages.** It created
all languages. There is no need to actually speak. **Silence
has its own language.** Aliens communicate telepathically
and that's what will happen to all people on Earth.

• **God / *The Creation* dwells within you.**
It is a spirit that dwells within your body and outside of it, in
everything. There is no point in seeking it out in material
objects, in distant lands, in the mountains, temples, bibles,
prayer houses, tombstones, or in ancient places.

• **All spirits belong to God / *The Creation.***
The quantity of spirits is limited.

All balls of light belong to God and exist forever and their
quantity is fixed in the universe.

■■

Governments dilute citizens with sterile vaccines such as Tetanus. The moment humanity on Earth gives birth using IVF technology, by manipulating nature via artificial pregnancy; they are 'stealing' spirits.
And if you know that what you do comes back to you, then the karma will return. Reduction of population is only a matter of time, by manipulating and frightening citizens to get vaccinated. There is a plan and order in the cosmos. Everything happens for a reason. The Creation is reducing the population to begin the Aquarius age with less quantity and more quality.

In order for a spirit to enter a body as a soul, then a soul from another body needs to exit in order to maintain the quantity of spirits balance. Each birth requires death.

■■

• The soul of the newborn enters its body only at birth, at the time it takes its first breath. **A situation in which two souls inhabit one living body is impossible.** The fetus feeds and breathes through the umbilical cord attached to its mother.

The soul of the fetus enters its body only when it is already outside the womb at the time of birth, when it takes its first breath.

• Human beings find it difficult to understand the world with endless limits and boundaries.
This is all too difficult for them to understand, so they created boundaries, limits, laws, measurements, times, quantities, sizes, territories, borders, etc.

The biblical story of Abraham and Sarah

These people are responsible for the ongoing karma between Arabs and Jews.
Abraham and his wife Sarah lived in ancient times in Egypt. The story tells how beautiful Sarah caused Abraham many problems. Pharaoh fell in love with Sarah, because of her beauty and when he found out that she was Abraham's wife, he banished them from Egypt to Canaan (Israel). There are no coincidences, because everything that happens, including exiles, is intended to serve a noble and good cause.

Sarah was barren, so she chose her handmaid, Hagar, to be Abraham's second wife. Hagar and Abraham had a son named Ishmael, which in Hebrew means: God will listen. "Ishma" = will listen and "El" = God.

After the birth of Ishmael, 90-year-old Sarah became 'miraculously' pregnant with the aid of the three messengers. She gave birth to Isaac, ('Itzhak') which in Hebrew means: will laugh.

Sarah acted out of jealousy at Hagar and Ishmael, then convinced Abraham, who was a very wealthy man, to banish them into the desert, with only a jug of water and bread, which he did.

Is that how a 'divine' father of Ishmael (Abraham) and a woman (Sarah) supposed to act? And still they are mentioned in the Jewish Torah as *"Abraham our father and Sarah our mother"*. Who the hell wants parents like these?

God tested Abraham and Sarah and they failed. Because of that, God sent messengers to save Hagar and Ishmael in the desert.

The meaning of the names Sarah and Hagar:

The name 'Sarah' (in Hebrew 'Zh'ara') means problem and a narrow point of view.

The name 'Hagar' (in Hebrew 'Lehager') means to migrate, and the word 'Gar' means foreigner.

• To this very day, Arabs, the descendants of Ishmael are angry about this injustice from the time their father, Abraham, who was a very wealthy man, gave Hagar and Ismael nothing but a jug of water and bread, to be left alone in the desert. Ishmael and Hagar were forced to migrate; they were sent into the desert in an unjust way and without any possessions.

• Ishmael represents the Arabs, who until this day live in desert countries and whom didn't receive respect, justice, inheritance, or birthright from their father Abraham and their brother Isaac, since then and up to nowadays.

The Arabs and the Jews are brothers from the same father, forever. Therefore, this karma will never end, until they will learn how to live together and respect each other, as brothers. This is a karma cycle that has gone on for thousands of years.

A biblical event will occur by *The Creation* and unite Arabs and Jews, by forcing a peace in the Middle-East, which will spread world-wide. This will happen starting from the year 2025, when the year of the light enters Earth. Justice and order will always be made by chaos first, in order to recreate, as *"every beginning requires chaos first."*

Abraham and Sarah
are the ancient ancestors
*of the **Jewish nation of Israel.***

Abraham and Hagar
are the ancient ancestors
*of the **Arab nations.***

The Jewish nation is the driving engine for
the Arab nations to rise up and lift themselves,
as they are brothers.

"Dear Arabs and Jews,
You are brothers; learn to live side by side
and respect one another."

"That which was not given in the past will be given!

For the problem will not be solved by the sword,
but with words of justice, recognition, and love".

How is it possible that a tiny country like Israel makes such global noise?

The Jewish nation designation is to bring light and message and to be an example around the world, in the same way that Jesus was a Jew, who brought a light and new message to the world, in favor of demolishing all religions. The karma must be fixed and Jesus will return to Earth in the upcoming era, in order to accomplish what wasn't done then.

■■■

Many corrupted powerful Jews world-wide are descendants of the **Khazarians from ancient Shumar (Iraq), calling themselves Zionists,** who hate Jews and hide behind Judaism, in order to annihilate them, as has happened throughout history (pogroms and holocaust).

Therefore, they built the Jewish Khazarian Zionist state in Israel, while they hide as Jews in government and all institutions, since the establishment of the state of Israel, in order to obliterate the Jews for good.

Every karma returns, in order to repair by chaos, until the Jewish citizens, who are victims, will be revealed to the shocking truth and eliminate the Khazarian Zionists from Israel and reorganize a new state name, flag, and national anthem, of their own, with the assistance of USA. **Israel will belong to United States of America.**

■■■

The moment there will be peace in Israel from the year 2025 on going, then peace will spread world-wide.

The Israeli nation should be admired, for taking many difficult roles upon themselves, such as bringing enlightenment, divine messages, awareness, peace, and insights to the rest of humanity, as Jesus did, as well as what this book does.

Insights about Life:

1. It is impossible to die, since you have an eternal spirit.

Internalize this insight and your fear of death will disappear, as your way of thinking will change, there won't be any reason to invest any more resources in armies, security, weapons, and wars. All resources will be available to serve the goals they were intended for:

• Non-satanic science and technology.
• Education, quality of life, and research.
• Protecting human rights and preserving animals and nature.
• Finding alternative natural resources of energy other than fuel, using air, pressure, and frequency - which is the symbol of the Aquarius from the Zodiac.

2. You don't invent anything because everything already exists. You've come to discover who you are, by understanding who you are not.

All the information, technology, knowledge, any new idea, or invention belongs to aliens and already existed in the past. Human beings simply reveal all this information from the past.

3. Nothing is yours; you are guests on planet Earth.
When you die, your soul leaves your body and returns as a ball of light to God / *The Creation*, while your spirit is stripped of all the assets, wealth, and relationships you had, but full of your insights, experiences, and memories from your previous life, which will continue with you to your next life form.

4. Planet Earth is the 'emotional planet'.
Planet Earth is navigated by the emotions of humankind. Being on planet Earth makes it difficult for souls in a human body to learn and survive.

Once you, as a ball of light enter a body, you become a soul. At the moment of death, the soul leaves the body and returns back to the bank of souls, and finally you return to your original state as a ball of light.

5. There are ten senses, rather than five senses.
Most human beings activate only five senses, instead of the ten senses, which is why they receive less information. This can lead to depression, suicidal tendencies, anger, self-destruction, and wars.

6. Each destiny contains main life lines and several parallel life lines.

Before a spirit entered your body and became a soul, **you wrote without ego your own destiny, which you chose to experience in a living form during each life time,** such as, which family you will belong to and in what location on Earth (country / city), including your physical appearance, language, gender, and your time of birth and death.
In your destiny, the main life lines are fixed, but the free will is given to human beings, by allowing them to choose the parallel destiny lines and time.

You have selected all of the above, in order to allow yourself a choice. This was out of a need to complete and correct that which you didn't have the chance to do in your previous incarnations.

7. Opposites were created in order to achieve balance and allow choice.

Man and woman, day and night, the devil and the white angel, heaven and hell, truth and lie, matter and spirit, sky and earth, and so on. If only one of these options existed, then you wouldn't have had the option to choose.

You have been given the ability to tell lies. **If lying was denied to you, then life on Earth would become very boring.** You wouldn't even enjoy a movie or a show, which are mostly based on fiction, made-up scripts, and performed by actors who memorize their lines (not referring to documentary).

8. There's no good and bad. Everything is relative.
What's good for one person, may not be good for another and vice versa. Therefore, there is no such thing as 'good or bad'. All is relative and for your own good, because everything that happens to you, will always benefit you in the future. **You are led by *The Creation* at every moment.**

9. As a ball of light you have no ego. The ego dwells in the physical body and is intended for survival. The lessons a human being must learn, is to control and balance the ego.

10. The greatness of humankind, is measured by compassion which is derived from tolerance, attentiveness, understanding, and helping the others.

Rules were dictated to humanity, by various members in the name of religion. Medical research indicates that a baby who is not touched and does not receive human love and warmth, will be negatively affected. This is because you are balls of light, who must receive the warmth of touch and love, in order to survive normally in a human body.

Christian believers:
1. Worship the pole on which Jesus was crucified and died. It's like worshipping a hanging rope or guillotine, which represent a negative energy of death. They are worshipping death, instead of life.

2. Mark the sign of the cross on their body, from the forehead, to the chest, and the shoulders, without understanding that they are marking an upside-down cross

which stands for the sign of the Satan. Each symbol in any religion or cult is idolatry.

All religions are on their way to vanish for good, because you don't need a mediator to reach God, which dwells inside you.

11. Competitions.
The very term 'competition' should not exist! Human beings who compete with one another, activate physical and mental strengths, and sometimes even cheat, in order to win. But who exactly are they beating?

Competitions were intended to separate humanity. Gain and loss cause the separation and the division of humanity. The right thing to do is to award certificates of participation or appreciation in a competition.

In beauty, culinary, or singing competitions, appearance, cooking or baking, and a good voice are judged according to a personal taste of a 'judge', whose preferences are of a particular period in time. What is beautiful, tasty, and pleasant to the ear for one person, may not be to others, so how can a so called 'judge' judge others?

In sports competitions, such as swimming, running, tennis, soccer, basketball, and so forth, is it really important to know which of the contestants has the better physical ability or which one of them paid a heavy price in his childhood and freedom, due to intense trainings, in order to 'win' a medal, trophy, and money?

Sports have become a money industry, missing the whole point of community, unity, and participation of society.

In intellectual competitions, such as math, physics, chess, Sudoku, trivia, and so forth, is it really important to discover who has better analytical capabilities?

The Nobel Prize is a corrupted organization, which acts similar to a mob! They choose only those who meet their standards and award them with money, certificates, and 'status'.

All these types of competitions have a pattern of divide and conquer, in order to separate the 'winner' from the 'loser', to enhance and glorify the ego of humankind.

12. Throughout our lives, we search for our other half. From the moment of your birth till the day you die, you are in a constant search to find your purpose and your twin soul, through love, academic or spiritual education, employment, travel, etc.

Chapter 3:
The basic rules of the universe

Rule No. 1 - Freedom of choice

Freedom of choice is given to all.

You were born naked with a soul that was lent to you from the bank of souls for your journey, inside a physical body. You receive life with the freedom of choice. **God/ *The Creation* will never deprive you from your freedom of choice; they are not allowed to choose for you.**

Always remember to allow freedom of choice to others. Never force anything against another's will. If you do so, you are eliminating their free-will (rule 1) and that will come back to you, because 'everything returns' (rule 2).

Every living being has a soul, then honor all living beings. All of nature around you is alive and contains a soul, including plants, animals, human beings, and more. All objects which are made from matter are alive, such as wood, glass, steel, paper, and so on, because their atoms move under a microscope.

You have the right to choose for yourself and for the helpless.

In case of helpless people, who are not in a conscious state to make wise decisions, such as children, the elderly, the sick, people with physical or mental disabilities, and animals, you must offer them as many choices as possible accompanied by advice and possible solutions, in order to allow them free choice, as if you were choosing for your own good. You should treat others, as you would like others to treat you. Everything you do, comes back to you.

If you abuse animals and nature,
then it will return to affect your life

Animal & nature rights

I asked the Entities the following question: *"Is it correct to slaughter animals for food?"*

Their response was: *"Only if there is nothing left to eat, because animals have souls".*

The Creation passes the decision to the human beings, to allow free choice.

Respect animals:

• **Do not stuff chickens** inside tiny and crowded coops, with 24 hours a day lighting, in order to enhance the production.

Chickens lay their eggs in great suffering and when a person eats those eggs or chickens, he absorbs their suffering, fear, and negative energy.

• **Do not separate** calves from their mothers, in order to produce veal (steak). **Do not fatten** geese. **Do not abuse,** beat, hunt, or starve animals.

• **Do not imprison animals in zoos or circus.** Their natural habitat is nature itself.

• **Do not pollute** drinking water, water sources, food, lands, air, and sky. Do not cut down too many trees. Do not overfish the oceans, and the list goes on and on.

*"Only a **quarter of animals**, just fish, may be eaten, as we are separating from the Pisces Age (fish Zodiac sign). Only **a quarter of crops** may be eaten. Only **a quarter of lands** can be used for living.* ***Any excessive consumption, will lead to shortages.****"*

Rule No. 2 - Everything returns

What goes around, comes around. Everything you do comes back to you. Due to gravity, you are attached to the ground of Earth, which is floating in space. Everything that surrounds you is alive. The universe is a whirlpool that turns around the stars and planets. The force of this cyclical movement makes everything go around.

The entire universe consists of circular rings, which expand and shrink, like human breathing.

Let's consider Einstein's formula and redefine it from the energetic aspect of the soul:

E = Energy = Consciousness or God / *The Creation.*

M = Mass of matter = Every material has a mass.

C = Constant speed of light = The source of all spirits is balls of light. In the universe there is more darkness than light. Therefore, you are able to measure the temporary light upon the darkness. In the universe, the darkness is permanent and the light is temporary.

I thought, I said, I acted = This is how you create energy.

Similar to the universe, when you think, speak, or act, that's how you create energy, because each act contains vibrations, which have dual energy.

Everything you do, comes back to you eventually, you are *The Creator* of your life.

The Circles of Creation

The entire universe is like a ping pong game, everything that is sent, returns back to the sender (rule No 2).

Negative thoughts

If you curse or cast a spell, then you create a vibration, an energy which is sent, reaches its destination, and then returns to you eventually. This bad energy might affect your health, success, relationships, livelihood, and more. That's why you must avoid cursing or wishing evil to others.

The karma will return to you, no matter if you did it, or someone else on your behalf for free or with payment, because the request came from you. Then, both you and the person who did the act, will be badly affected in this lifetime, because 'everything returns' (rule No. 2).

Positive thoughts

If you bless, support or send love, then you create a vibration, an energy, which reaches its destination and returns to you for the better, because everything you do comes back to you. (rule No 2).

Do good deeds and perform acts of kindness; this has nothing to do with religion, but with creating your own life paths.

Here are some cycles of creation through spoken sentences: *"I have **no** job, I have **no** career, I have **no** love, I will **never** be employed..."*

In these words, you send a vibration, an echo to the universe and at the same moment, you establish a fact which returns to you, because *'I have no'* will bring *'I have no'!*
Therefore, instead of saying 'I have no' or 'I don't have', say: *"I'm about to have a job, career, love, good prosperity, and so on".*

There are two universal rules:

• Freedom of choice (rule No.1)

• Everything returns (rule No.2)

These rules are interconnected in an endless cycle.

• **God / *The Creation* will never choose for you.**
Your every action is done out of free choice (rule 1), which activates self-creation (thought, speech, and action) and returns back to you (rule 2) and so on.

| Rule 1:
Freedom of choice | | Rule 2:
All returns |

Before you as a ball of light enter a body and become a soul

• You select the main and secondary life lines of your destiny for your current incarnation, which you choose without ego before you are born, in order to allow you several options.

• You can choose to be born with a disability, to undergo traumas, diseases that you will suffer throughout your life, because the spirit selects its destiny, without ego before birth.

• In difficult times, the tendency of a person is to withdraw within himself, to lose trust and to feel frustration, as a victim, without understanding that all the 'bad things' that happen to him, are only for his own good, lessons which he chose to undergo in his current lifetime.

The life lines

1. Human beings possess free choice.

Even after a person is given a prediction of the future, he still possesses free choice, in order to fulfill his goals in the way he chooses. The decision to act and to fulfill these goals depends only on the person himself and this influences the future's prediction. If a person chooses not to fulfill the prediction which he received, then the universe will bring him new challenges at a different timeline.

In other words, everything which is about to happen, will be postponed or may be fulfilled earlier, or even canceled, depending on the person's actions and choices.

A fixed main destiny life line exists for every person, yet secondary life lines move in parallel and change according to the person's choices.

Therefore, predictions will never be 100% accurate, because they are only correct at the time of the prediction, as the life lines always change, based on the person's decisions.

2. Those who deal with the spiritual world are human beings without any 'superpower'.
There are spiritual people with prediction abilities, who use most of their 10 senses. Predicting the future is not a simple task, it involves maneuvering between predicting to a person and allowing him the free choice.

God / *The Creation* prevented human beings from seeing and predicting everything, so they will not lose interest in life. God will never reveal everything, because once it's hidden, *The Creation's* engine will push people to search and find, however it is a game which will never end, because the power will always be in the hidden, as God. Once you reveal everything, then the game is over, which is why there will never be a single truth. The mystery is what keeps humanity active and awake. **The ability to predict the future is**

limited in order to preserve the freedom of choice, curiosity, and the element of surprise and curiosity.

Everything is foreseen, yet free-will exists

'Everything is foreseen'

You were born naked with a soul which was lent to you, main and secondary life lines, and freedom of choice. God / *The Creation* will never decide for you, you die only when you choose to die.

The main destiny life line is fixed and never changes *(everything is foreseen).*

Before a spirit enters a body, it chooses:

• The location, in which the person will be born.

• The time, in which the spirit will enter and leave the body (birth and death).

• The gender of the person in a human body.

• The person's family members, and so on.

The fixed main destiny life line and the secondary life lines are moving together and parallel to one another, crossing intersections, which were chosen in advance by the spirit.

'Yet free will exists'
The secondary life lines are constantly changing.
As gates open and close (*since free will exists*).

Gates exist within the secondary life lines and **provide opportunities**, which you can implement in your life. Nothing will happen, unless you act to achieve it.

Like changing stations, these gates offer you several options and times for each decision in your life. You must choose wisely, there are no coincidences.

Everything that happens is always for your best interest. Even if you have failed, it's a sign that you were supposed to experience in order to correct.

Sometimes, people see themselves as 'victims of life'. They live their lives filled with self-pity out of ego, stubbornness, and laziness. They do not try to change or to select a secondary life line, a different option, or a different gate.

They may use the aid of spiritual people, who can provide them with tools, answers, and insights. But the actions must be taken by the person, in order to change his life.

God helps those who help themselves.
God loves all his children across the universe, even those who get lost and are found by divine messengers from God.

People who see themselves as victims, choose to ignore and don't understand the source of their problems. **They choose to live in their past, without building their future** and create dependency and burden on the society via self-destruction.

Their condition is not going to improve, unless they choose to help themselves. God / *The Creation* will help only those who begin to help themselves and will assist the ones who let go of their ego, listen, respect the others, and wish to change their lives.

The free choice of the soul, allows you to select a new path at any time. In your life, you can switch, change, move forward, or remove difficulties, according to your free will.

If everything was known in advance,
then you could not have free choice.
God / The Creation will not dictate,
*but rather **allow you to choose for yourself**.*
Even if your choices are wrong,
you learn through your experience.

Chapter 4:
You cannot die

Spirits, balls of light, and souls are the source of life. They exist forever and cannot die, but can change their state, and their destiny is to testify to the nature of God / *The Creation* through the actions of humanity. When a ball of light dwells in a human body, it becomes a soul. Only at the moment of death the soul returns to the bank of souls and then to its original state, as ball of light. Each living body serves as a vessel, through which the soul can manifest as matter and walk in the physical dimension on Earth.

You are an eternal spark of God / The Creation.
The soul, in its original state as a ball of light,
breathes life into a temporary physical body
and returns to its spiritual state at the time of death.
You have no beginning and no end.
Everything is eternal.

Death

Each death is a temporary transit station, in the course of infinite life. **You cannot and will not die, you only change a host body.**

You as a ball of light select a human body and breathe life into it by renting a soul, which enters the body during birth at the second breath of the newborn and exits the body at the time of death, in order to complete your lessons and destiny, which you chose before being born. After death, the soul exits your body and returns to the bank of souls and then begins its journey back 'home' to God / *The Creation* as a ball of light. You are eternal.

Life cannot be stopped

You cannot destroy anything, but you can change the state of matter:

• Each tree or grass you uproot, every leaf or fruit that you pluck, will grow again.

• Every forest you burn down and every lake or sea you pollute, will eventually renew itself.

• Each planet that explodes in space, will simultaneously create the seeds of stardust, out of which new stars will be created. You cannot destroy or kill anything, because everything lives forever and in cyclicality.

The right to die

Everything that ends, has chosen to end.
Every person who died, his soul chose it.
No-one is forced to die.
Everything chose its moment of birth and death.

You must not prevent a person from ending his own life, which he received from and is able to return to God. You must not incarcerate and drug a person with medication, in order to 'preserve his life', while the person is no longer interested in being in the body it selected.

When a person asks to end his life, it is important to listen to him, understand his motives, and advise him otherwise, without forcing him, **yet still give him the option to die.**

It is the right of everyone to end its journey at any time, in order to start over in a new body or form.

Birth and death

In order for a ball of light to enter the body of a fetus (birth), a soul must be chosen from the bank of souls and breathe life into a living body, as another soul exits another body (death).
The universe always maintains a balance.
The birth of one person is the death of another.
You cannot gain life without another loss of life.

That is why both states must be celebrated:

• At the time of birth, we celebrate the entry of the ball of light as a soul into a body.

• **At the time of death**, we celebrate the departure of the soul from the body and the return of you as ball of light to God.

You as a ball of light came to Earth to dwell in a living body, in order to have emotional experiences, to correct karmas from previous incarnations and to testify to your nature, and by that to the nature of God / *The Creation.*

All knowledge is taught by studying its opposite. In other words:

• How can you appreciate light, unless you have experienced darkness?

• How will you know to appreciate success, unless you have experienced failure?

• How can you appreciate money or family, unless you have lost them?

• How can you appreciate love, until you have experienced loss or disappointment?

• How can you appreciate life, unless you have lost the life of others, or lost parts of your bodily functions?

The four stages of death

1. The first stage: Exiting the body

The soul **separates itself** from the body and the ego, and returns to the bank of souls and then returns to God in its original state as ball of light.

You look at the body from the outside and realize that you are experiencing 'death', with much confusion, knowing you no longer dwell inside the body, but separate from it.

God asks each one of you to choose whether to move on with the journey of life or rather return back to the physical body. God / *The Creation* will never take life, without your permission. In order to die, a living form must choose to do so.

If you **choose to return** to the body you left, you will be sucked back into the body and will experience physical pain during the process.

2. The second stage: The corridor of light

You will experience tremendous frequency of love and must seek to find *'the corridor of light'* without fear.

As you enter *'the corridor of light',* someone will be waiting for you there, such as a relative, friend, or any another person you chose to meet. This depends on the **faith**, which you have accumulated during your life in a body:

▪ **If you believe** in reincarnation, you will be able to watch parts of your previous life and realize who you were.

▪ **If you believe** that relatives and loved ones who have passed away will be waiting for you, then this is what you will experience.

▪ **If you believe** that a spiritual or religious entity or even aliens will arrive to greet you, then this is what you will experience.

▪ **If you believe** that you will meet *God / The Creation,* then this is what you will experience.

▪ **If you believe** that you deserve to be punished (thanks to you being an ego-free spirit) and to suffer in Hell for your misdeeds, then this is what you will experience.

▪ **If you believe** that you were a good person and deserve to reach Heaven, then this is what you will experience. Hell and Heaven only exist in your imagination, because once you imagine, you create.

▪ **If you do not believe** in the spiritual world, in *God / The Creation,* then you will not notice it, even after your death, in the same way you did not notice it during your lifetime in a body. You will skip this stage and immediately be transferred to the third stage.

3. The third stage: self-judgment without ego

As you pass over, you will give yourself a 'fair-trial', **without an ego or judging yourself:**

"What have you done during your lifetime inside a body?

How have you helped yourself and others and what contribution have you left behind?

What have you learned, what education or insights have you acquired for yourself?

What destiny and karma have you completed?"

God / *The Creation* is all love, and therefore there is no *'wrath and fury of God'* or *'Chariots of the Gods'*, those are superstitions from folk tales, which were born out of the need to control people by intimidation.

4. The fourth stage: Unification

You will continue to experience a tremendous frequency of love on your way 'back home' as a ball of light to be unified with God / *The Creation.* The moment you reach the end of your spiritual journey inside a living body, then you will spiritually ascend and will achieve **'enlightenment'**, and if not, you will continue your journey as a spirit and enter / dwell in a living body or remain as a spirit and become a spiritual entity. It depends on the level of 'spiritual hierarchy' you have reached.

Return from death

At the moment of death, when the soul leaves the body, it returns to the bank of souls and you return to God as **ball of light.**

There are cases, in which the spirit chooses to have a second chance, as described below: At the time of death, you as a spirit undergo the first stage, in which you are asked whether you choose to return to the body or to continue on as a spirit. If you as a spirit choose at that stage to return to the body which you inhabited, then you will quickly be sucked back into the body and will experience physical pain.

In most cases, people who choose to return back into their body, suffer with mental health issues, try to reach for answers, are misunderstood by others, and feel lonely. Therefore, it is not wise to request to prolong your date of death. **At the moment you start changing your timeline destiny plan, you cause problem to yourself.**

Clinical death

People have experienced clinical death, when their rented souls exit their body. Miraculously, each person gave a different description of his experience. This is because **they experienced and viewed their 'own state of being', which they had created for themselves.**
Not even God, but only you choose for yourself the time of your death, whether you want to return back to your body again, or to continue as a spirit in your life journey.

Suicide

The first rule is freedom of choice. *God / The Creation* will never interfere with your choices. **Remember, you are an endless spirit as a ball of light, you can never die.**

In the same way that you can choose to be born, you are also allowed to choose when to die and temporarily pause your journey as a spirit inside a living body.

Your lives were lent to you, in the same way that a book is borrowed from the library. You decide when you will return the book to the *'Library of The Creation'.*

• People who choose to commit suicide, after death their spirit as a ball of light returns home to God, they will be surrounded by love, **and will never be** abandoned, or sent to hell if they did not ask for it. **God never punishes, only you judge yourself, without ego, at the moment of death.**

• People who committed suicide, chose to let go of their lives after a tremendous spiritual or physical ordeal, which made it difficult for their soul to cope as soul inside a human body. These people have suffered enough, therefore God / *The Creation* won't punish them again, but love them with deep understanding, compassion, and allow them to choose to experience physical life again, in their next incarnation, in order to help them finish their lessons.

• People who committed suicide, most likely have suicided before in their previous incarnations. They will need to experience the same dilemmas again and again, until they will finish their karma by not committing suicide. It's like a person who fails a driver's license test over and over, until he passes the test and then the karma is over. Everything in life is lessons, and God will always give you the opportunity to change, without regard for time, for as long as it takes. Sometimes people may need to undergo thousands of incarnations, until they complete and achieve their lessons.

You should not judge and disrespect people who chose to take their own life, as it's theirs. For example, the Jewish religion should not bury people who commit suicide in a different section within the cemetery, as if they were not equal to others.

Coma

A coma is a state, in which the soul is temporarily separated from the living body, and stays connected to it with a string. **During a coma, the soul discusses with *The Creation* whether to return to the physical body or detach itself and return home to God as a ball of light.**

A person in a coma, will not experience any physical pain, but his soul is aware of its state, hears and sees all that is happening to the body, in the physical dimension. For example, a person might be in a coma state for four years, but in reality, only a week has passed, because the 'time' in the universe does not match the time on Earth, which was created by humans.

Artificial respiration

Connecting a sick or a coma patient to respiratory machines is done out of the genuine concern of his relatives, and the medical staff to act according to their oath, to do everything in their power to extend life artificially. But, do they have the right to interfere with the course of nature?

In order to make this dilemma easier for his loved ones to understand, it is recommended to involve a spiritual medium or healer who can channel with the patient's soul, to receive and confirm the soul's wish.

During life, it's best to prepare a 'living will' in which you express your 'final life requests'. The medical staff and the person's relatives must honor and comply with the person's request if he or she chooses not to be connected to the respiratory machines.

If the medical staff or the person's relatives do not grant the patient's request, then they are denying from him the first rule, 'freedom of choice', which is the freedom to choose to be born and when to die.

At the same time, they activate the second rule, 'Everything returns', so then as a karma, the freedom will be taken, from the medical staff and / or the patient's relatives, because everything you do comes back to you.

Euthanasia

Nowadays, euthanasia is intended only for terminally ill patients in a few countries. There is no 'mercy' in that act, because the medical staff is supposedly 'doing a merciful act', in which they are simply performing **the person's natural free will to die and return to God as a ball of light.**

A message to the medical staff:

"You who have been chosen to treat patients,
You must demonstrate patience, attentiveness, and care;
respect people and their freedom of choice.
Do not burden them with examinations and medicine.
Use your emotional intelligence and intuition.
You must use the assistance of mediums and healers.
People are sick because of your actions, the vaccines,
drugs, and all the medical satanic industry which makes
money from sickness and helps governments to depopulate
the masses in order to control and survive.
Remember that everything you do comes back to you now,
during your lifetime".

Trapped souls

There are cases during death, in which a soul leaves the body and becomes a spirit, but for various reasons cannot find or enter the corridor of light. Such a spirit hasn't reached a decision yet, regarding whether it should return to the body or leave it for good.

A soul that has left the physical body, becomes a spirit, which has not yet entered the corridor of light, **still exists as a spirit**, **ghost,** until it chooses to move forward and complete the four stages of death, in order to gain a new form of life.

Out of fear, anger, and frustration, trapped spirits are able to harass living people, animals, and even cause physical damage to properties. The actions of these spirits are a call for help and mediums are able to assist them to enter the corridor of light, in order to gain a new form of life.

Question: *"Why doesn't God help trapped spirits return home to him?"*

Answer: *"In all stages of death, God / The Creation will never interfere, in order to allow all the free will to choose."*

Heaven and hell

You cannot die. Death is a temporary station in the journey of the spirit. At the moment of death, the soul departs itself from the living body and ego, and returns to the bank of souls and then returns to its original state as a ball of light. From that point, **you judge yourself and every decision is pure and ego-free.**

If you realize that you deserve to go to heaven, this is what you will experience.

If you realize that you have done wrong and deserve to be 'punished' and 'sent to hell', this is what you will experience.

Heaven and hell do not exist in reality. They are not a physical place, but a state of mind, because the moment you imagine, you create. Thanks to the first rule, 'free will', heaven and hell look different to each spirit.

When you reach heaven, you will find a place filled with spectacular natural sights, infinite beauty and marvelous light, filled with love and happiness. Each one will experience this place differently, according to their spiritual and energy level.

When you reach hell, you will find a quiet place, nobody burns; you will be secluded and will think about your previous acts and mistakes, and experience a kind of spiritual suffering, but not actual physical suffering, because as a spirit you don't have a physical body, which means that:

• You will watch yourself from the side, and notice yourself 'suffering', until you will understand your mistakes, so that you can choose wisely and make corrections in your next incarnation. Each one will experience hell differently, according to their spiritual and energetic level.

• The moment you realize that your stay in hell is no longer meaningful, and you no longer need to 'suffer', then you will move on to the fourth stage of death and merge with God, in order to be able to gain a living form again.

The Devil / Prince of Darkness exists in order to allow all in the infinite universe, with the free will to choose. **Satan is sent by God to test all forms of life.**
There isn't good or bad, because it's all relative, and in order to deeply understand, you must ask both sides.
For example, if someone is suffering and asks a person to help him die, is it considered a murder or is it simply a fulfillment of the suffering person's free will?
Nowadays, unfortunately laws do not respect the free will of the person who chose to die.

The stars, the sun, and the moon emit light without interruption throughout the day. The Earth allows only half of the planet to be exposed to sunlight half of the day, in order to balance, rest and provide humanity with darkness, for sleep and relaxation. Perhaps a temporary stay in hell is a necessary lesson for a spirit, which still did not learn its lessons and did not realize what mistakes it had made in previous incarnations. There are no coincidences, everything is always for the spirit's benefit.

Darkness was here long before the light. The whole universe exists in darkness. The purpose of light is to discover that which already exists in darkness.
From the darkness, you were created, and to the darkness you shall return. Accept the darkness as a background color, upon which you shine, with your own light.

The ten senses

In the light, the five physical senses are active.

In the darkness, the other five supernatural senses are active. They are not revealed in the physical dimension, but rather in the spiritual one. In order to experience these senses, you only need to shut your eyes and connect with your intuition and imagination.

Most people activate the five physical senses through their body:
1. The sense of **touch.**
2. The sense of **taste.**
3. The sense of **smell.**
4. The sense of **sight.**
5. The sense of **hearing**.

If you add the word 'supernatural' to the abovementioned physical senses, then you obtain the five supernatural senses, which are activated by the intuition, which is being affected directly by the chakras and the auras:

1. The supernatural sense of **touch (sensation).**

2. The supernatural sense of **taste.**

3. The supernatural sense of **smell.**

4. The supernatural sense of **sight.**

5. The supernatural sense of **hearing.**

This is how your reach a total of **ten senses.**

All ten senses send knowledge vibrations
to the intuition, which can be strengthened by
constant practice, without fear.
It is amusing to call them 'supernatural senses',
when they are so natural and exist
within the intuition of each human being.

Chapter 5: Burial

Death and birth

You cannot die.

Physical death is only a 'temporary stage' in the spirit's endless journey as a ball of light.

In order to walk in the physical dimension, the spirit as a ball of light must breathe life into a temporary physical body, as a soul.

At the time of death, the soul departs from the physical body it inhabits and returns as a spirit back to the bank of souls and then to its original state as ball of light. The only thing that you possess is your freedom of choice.

During preparation for birth, people make arrangements and prepare for the labor. Sometimes they hire the services

of a childbirth instructor or midwife, who accompanies the
mother or the couple through the process.

During preparation for death, people prepare their living
will, but avoid preparing themselves or their loved ones
mentally for death. They should do that, by using mediums,
healers, religious people, any other person or animal, in
order to prepare themselves for their final stage, as all living
beings experience it.

*It is important to mentally prepare a person
for his death, with the help of an instructor,
who provides knowledge, removes fears, and prepares
the person for his final stage in each incarnation, as you
cannot die.*

World-wide there aren't many clinics which support and
prepare mentally, the terminally ill people for death.

You must get rid of your fear of death, by receiving the right
knowledge. Death is a part of the natural lifecycle of every
living being. In order for a spirit to enter the body of a fetus,
at the time of birth, another soul must leave a different body.
Each moment of birth, is also a moment of death for another.

Do not fear death

Each spirit as a ball of light chooses to rent a soul and enter
into a physical body in a physical dimension, in order to
complete its lessons, to ascend energetically, up to
enlightenment, as each act testifies to the nature of God.

At the time of death, when you depart from your body, you will feel an immense sense of relief, freedom, and mainly the divine frequency of love.

If you reach new insights, then you will not fear death.

You will know when to choose to die. Choose death at a time that's suitable for you. There are many people who suffer in their physical body, but do not let go of it and remain suffering in it, just because of their fear from death. This does not mean that you should commit suicide or take your own life.

Burial methods

"Dust to dust and ashes to ashes..."

Every physical body must return to nature as it is a part of it and be cremated instead of buried in the ground.

In most of Asia, the body is cremated, which is wise, in order to conserve lands. Most of Earth is covered by water. This is why lands are a scarce resource and must be used by the living, and not be wasted by buried corpses. At the end of the cremation ceremony, the ashes may be scattered back into nature or placed in urns, according to the request of the deceased or his relatives.

In most of the developed countries, the body is buried in lands or in walls, with or without a coffin, and with a gravestone.

This is NOT wise, because:
• In general, burial is more expensive than cremation.
• It is a waste of valuable land, which should be used by the living.

"Thou shalt not make unto thee any graven image..."

Idolatry

Purchasing a burial spot involves considerable cost, depending on the location, type of stone and decorations.

The grave might turn into a pilgrimage site, which is similar to idolatry. Sometimes, these rituals might lead to family arguments, based on who did and didn't arrive to the ceremony.

The moment the gravestone is placed on the burial spot, it officially becomes a pilgrimage site, by visiting the gravesite after a month, once a year, and is known as the annual memorial service. Each visit to the bloody stone may turn into a 'family event', which includes inviting people, meals and gatherings, eulogies and prayers, with or without a member of the clergy, who usually charges a fee for his services.

Matter will never be holy, but only life and spirit. Only the things that you are not able to see through your eyes, but with your faith, are holy. **Because of this, religion can never be holy, as it deals with matter. Only free faith, which allows free will, is holy.**

Therefore, each person who disrespects the freedom of others, disrespects himself, disrespects the holy spirit of God's creations, and this energy will come back to haunt him during his lifetime.

Chapter 6:
Health

Migraine

A migraine mostly affects women, because women originate from the aliens, therefore they naturally receive information through channeling and are more open-minded to assimilate insights, innovate ideas, and practice spirituality, than men.

A migraine is a state of receiving information via channeling, which remains stuck in the head, because the knowledge is not transferred. This process is received from the crown chakra at the top of the head, to the third eye between the eyebrows, and projects onto the forehead and temples and may cause physical pain and pressure until it subsides.

This is the reason migraines have no scientific explanation or cure. Every disfunction of the physical body originates from the soul. Most medicines do not cure, not even migraines, but only anesthetize the pain temporarily, because the origin of migraines is spiritual.

All vaccines are toxic and disrupt a person's natural immune system. Migraine is also a phenomenon of vaccine toxins such as cancer, autism, OCD, epilepsy and all other diseases caused by deliberate government poisoning from the sky, water, agriculture, consumer products, and medicine.

How to deal with a migraine

The moment a migraine attacks, one option is to start writing down everything that pops into your mind. At first, only random meaningless sentences will appear, until messages begin to emerge, depending on your positive thinking, without fear, just believe in yourself.

The second option is to practice meditation, yoga, and learn how to use your intuition and channel, which may help.

Obsessive-Compulsive Disorder (OCD)

This type of mental disorder mostly affects people who are good, perfectionists, and over-sensitive to their environment.

People with OCD, adopt rules and behaviors for themselves, in order to perform certain rituals, which will protect them and keep them safe, from stress and flood of information. They are afraid to lose their balance or go mad.

The root causes

The root cause of OCD is related to fears and may have started at childhood or past incarnations. OCD can also be passed on genetically through DNA or as a result of:

• A crisis in their personal life and stress.

• Being perfectionists and not being able to achieve a goal; having high standards, which are difficult to meet.

• Lack of sleep, abuse, and negative self-worth thinking.

Some people with OCD have reached a crisis and a turning point in their lives, following a traumatic event. Many of them have constant destructive, bothersome, or damaging thoughts, without being able to stop this draining loop, out of fear that a 'disaster' might take place if they do so, for which they will feel responsible and blame themselves. This is why they are considered sensitive, caring, and thoughtful of their surroundings.

Their brain does not allow them to release the cycle. In order to help them, **mainly using mediums,** it's important to understand **the source of their problem,** which may have originated in their past incarnations, and what they went through in this current life.

Every mental issue starts from the spiritual world. Psychologists and psychiatrists only deal with the material world, and depend on what the patient reveals to them, without having the ability to know whether it's false or true. These professionals do not receive direct information regarding the patient's previous incarnations and current life from *The Creation*, as a medium can.

Tips for reducing OCD

Use a notebook, mobile phone or recording device and document each bothersome thought in it, include the date, time, and number of times it appeared. Once you document and remind yourself, it will help you not to repeat it.

The moment an action is performed or a disturbing repeating thought comes to mind, it should be documented, for example:
"Date / Time: Sep 20, 20xx, 10:12 am.

I closed the door, and verified that it is closed."

"Date / Time: Jan 4, 20xx, 11:30 am.
I washed my hands with soap, and verified they're clean."

"Date / Time: May 10, 20xx, 5:03 pm.
A disturbing thought is currently on my mind and now I
will describe and document it..."

Once it has been documented, you are safe and there is no need to repeat it.

** **Note:** The abovementioned is by no means a medical advice, but simply tips and opinions. In case of any medical, mental, or psychological problem, one should consult with the proper health care professional, in order to receive treatment and counseling.

The mentally ill

'A healthy soul, in a healthy body'.

Every pain originates in the soul, which is reflected mentally and / or on the physical body.

People cannot be cured using only conventional medicine,
because the soul, spirit, is the one that is ill.
Medicine can only anesthetize, blur, and remove
the problem temporarily, but cannot fully cure it.

The mentally ill do not control their ability to experience their ten senses, and are able to hear voices and see images, mainly because their halos are torn. Mostly, it's not their imagination, because once you imagine, you create.

Human beings are surrounded by seven halos, in order to balance and protect the body from the outside.

When halos are damaged and torn, as a result of crisis and depression, then a person loses his mental balance and begins to experience most of the ten senses, without having the tools to control or balance them.

A message for Psychologists, Doctors, and Advisors

"You make a living from the illnesses of patients, you serve a satanic infrastructure of governments to control citizens and make them sick and drug users, by brainwashing with fear to make them 'the same', by intimidation, inventing diseases and epidemics, killing citizens with vaccines, drugs and medical procedures.

Remember that everything you do will come back to you in your current life time.

In addition, you do not understand anything about what is the destiny, the lesson, and the karma that each patient came to finish during his life time, otherwise he would not have been born. The purpose is to rise up from the material body into the spiritual form. Therefore, your jobs will be eliminated in favor of mediums, healers, and extraterrestrial technology for faster healing, without any drugs, hospitals, clinics, and pharmaceutical companies".

During sleep the soul leaves the body, in which it dwells, in order to rest, connect, and recharge from the spiritual world, to which it belongs. When the soul leaves the body, it is connected by a 'thin silver string' to the navel. The soul's travels are translated into dreams. The soul returns to the body, right before the sleeping person awakens.

While sleeping, the soul is temporarily outside and connected to the human body. **The moment you frighten or bother a sleeping person**, you might cause him fear, restlessness, and even anger. Lack of sleep, may lead to extreme mental damage and madness.

Opening the chakras

There are those who turn to spiritual advisors, in order to open their chakras in an artificial way, like opening the third eye. This act is not recommended due to the following:

• **Opening the chakras artificially, may activate the ten senses all at once rather than gradually,** which might open the ability to hear voices, smell scents, and see visions, colors, deceased, aliens, and entities, without any control.

• Chakras that were opened, cannot be closed automatically, but can only be closed by the person himself with the aid of spiritual advisors.

• The chakras are energetic circular muscles, that can be opened and closed by using imagination. In order to close chakras, you may practice imagining the chakras becoming smaller, until they get closed.

Illness

Illness at a young age

Everyone is created healthy when the parents are healthy without vaccinations. **God does not make mistakes when he creates**. Every child who is born is being injected with toxic vaccines in a hospital and during his life, in order to disrupt his health, to become sick and in-need of medicine, thus financially supporting the pharmaceutical companies and the doctors, and he is no longer a danger to governments because sick patients do not rebel. In the Pisces Age which we are separating from, everything was done in medical fraud under the guise of strengthening the immune system, when the population became too loyal to the governments, doctors, and too stupid to investigate for themselves.

Sometimes children get ill or die at an early age, because their spirit needs to experience a lesson in a human body, in order to understand and **appreciate the value of life**, which was not accomplished in the child's previous incarnations, as the child may have been involved with destroying, killing, wounding, abusing, stealing, or controlling others.

In most cases, **the soul will choose to value life,** as it suffers from an illness, pain, or defect, in order to ascend to a higher energy level of the spirit.

*Sometimes the life of the soul within the physical body, will be short. You cannot be born or die **unless you chose** to do so. God will not give you life or take it from you, unless you ask for it.*

Remember: **you cannot die.** Before the spirit enters a human body as a soul in each incarnation, it chooses how to make a closure.

Illness at an older age

As mentioned above under the illnesses at a young age, everyone is created healthy when the parents are healthy without vaccinations. **God does not make mistakes when he creates**. Every person who is born is being injected with toxic vaccines in a hospital and during this life, in order to disrupt his health, to become sick and in need of medicine, thus financially supporting the pharmaceutical company and the doctors and he is no longer a danger to governments because sick patients do not rebel. In the Piscean age which we are separating, everything was done in medical fraud of strengthening the immune system when the population became too loyal to the governments, doctors and too stupid to investigate for them self.

Most people become sick with old age, because governments vaccinate with toxins since birth, pollute the drinking water with toxins and fluoride, spray chemicals in the sky and in agriculture, allow the consumption of industrialized and toxic food products, toxic smoking, and more. It's a wonder we're still alive at an old age.

Most doctors do not deal with the soul, the source of the problem, but only physically diagnose and write drug prescriptions, similar to drug dealers, in order to keep you seek and keep their jobs, to enrich themselves and the pharmaceutical companies that pay them back, and to help governments to depopulate and control the masses.

All that belongs to the Pisces Age from which we are separating, and all the corrupted people will disappear when humanity enters the Age of Aquarius. More than vaccinated people, corrupted people will die.

The majority of doctors, hospitals, and clinics are funded by the big pharma industry and world health organizations, which are responsible for creating and maintaining diseases and pandemics with patent numbers, in order to control, make a profit, and help governments reduce population. It's an evil combination.

Governments are terrified from the masses, who can take them down. You have to understand in what a crooked world you are currently living in. But, thanks to the karma in the universe, everything you do comes back to you. Therefore, in the coming years, all corrupted people, organizations, and governments, including big pharma, hospitals, clinics, and most doctors and medical staff, will be gone for good and replaced with mediums, healers, frequency medicine and devices, DNA repair, and advanced alien medical technology.

If technology and the big pharma advanced medicines are supposed to improve life, then how come the number of patients and hospitals around the world is growing each year?

Vaccinations

All vaccinations are toxic and were created to maintain people sick, that help the governments to control their population growth, and reduce the number of their citizens. We have reached an age in which big pharma and world health organizations are controlling governments, which control their citizens, all by using fake pandemics.
Once you control health, then you control the world. But, once people will understand you cannot die, all that corruption will end.

· ·

If you choose to be vaccinated, you are sending a message to God, saying: *"I don't believe in what you have created, therefore I need to improve myself, which means I don't believe in myself, in the body you gave me, and I don't believe in you God."*

· ·

Throughout history, parents unknowingly vaccinated their children, which ruined their natural body given by God. Unfortunately, over time their children developed deformities, diseases, autism, celiac, obesity, allergy symptoms, diabetes, and more. These parents were deceived, by the Satanic health system and the government, to intentionally cause damage to their children. **That's why the karma will return, after thousands of years to awaken the masses and eliminate all that is corrupted.**

Chapter 7:
Life & Soul

Life

• It is **a great privilege** for the physical body, once a soul breathes life into it.

• **Life is the only sacred thing. Not books, tombstones, people, or religions. Matter can never be sacred. Nothing is sacred except life, soul, spirit, and you as a ball of light.**

• In order to be born, the spirit must choose to do so, and in order to die, the person must choose as well.

God / *The Creation* will not take life without permission. **Only the person makes the decision** whether to continue to dwell in a body or return to God.

• **The mission of all souls in the living body** is to testify about themselves, and by that testify to the nature of God / *The Creation*.

The Soul

• There cannot be a situation, in which two souls occupy the body of a single pregnant woman during pregnancy.

• When a newborn baby takes its first breath, only then **the spirit enters the body and dwells in it as a soul.** Therefore, the fetus in its mother's womb is still without a soul. The fetus feeds and breathes through the umbilical cord of his mother.

• The soul does not have an ego. At the moment the soul enters a living body, it receives ego for survival purposes.

• **The soul is in every living thing,** such as the air, water, plants, animals, human beings, aliens, and so on. The spirit can choose to breathe life into a body, or to remain a spirit, as ball of light..

Remember the spiritual rule: *If you don't see it, it doesn't mean it doesn't exist.* In order to see beyond, you must imagine and practice the ten senses.

• You as ball of light, as a spirit has no beginning and no end. The time that the soul stays in each body is short, compared to its infinite lifetime as a spirit.

• The moment of death is joyous and liberating for the soul, which was trapped inside the body. Every physical death is a transit station from the material to the spiritual.

During sleep

• The soul experiences freedom when the body is sleeping. It leaves the body, attaches to the navel with a thin silver cord, hovers as a soul in the spiritual world, travels back and forward through time, and then returns to the body before it awakens.

• This is why you should not scare people who are asleep, because it might cause them trauma, such as damage to the auras, fears, problems with memory and concentration, and even madness.

Prolonging life

You cannot die. You are eternal.
You can always choose to dwell in a different form, such as in a spiritual or physical body.

Prolonging life artificially in hospitals against a person's wishes goes against the first rule 'the freedom of choice'.

The right thing to do:

1. If a conscious person asks to end his own life, due to a severe illness or any other reason, then he is entitled to do so.

2. In a case of an unconscious person (coma), it would be wise to consult with spiritual people, such as mediums, in order to understand the wish of the person, regarding whether he would like to continue living. This person will be connected

to artificial respiration, **only** if he requested and documented it prior to being unconscious. Remember that without the artificial equipment, in a natural state, the soul would have left the body earlier.

3. Each person must prepare for himself during his life a living will with his 'final life requests'.

4. It is wise to advise a person who wishes to die and provide him consultation, but not to decide for him, in order to provide him with a free will to choose. Otherwise, the second rule 'Everything returns' will automatically be activated as karma, and return back to those who chose for him.

5. People who ask to end their lives and commit suicide, mostly ended their life in previous incarnations, and cyclically returned to life again and again, in order for them to choose life instead of death, which is part of their main lessons.

Despite of Rule No. 1, which allows humans with free will, it is not recommended that people commit suicide, because the act itself will not solve the problem, but will become a karma issue, until it will be solved.

Every difficulty in life, is a test from God to you.
It's unlikely that people will kill themselves over any type of test in life, such as a driver's license test, an academic test, or a training test, etc.

When someone experiences difficulty, he needs to reach to the community or other people who will gladly help him.

This is why we are here for on Earth, to help each other.
Everything you do comes back to you, in this lifetime.
Once you help others, you are helping yourself.

The book of life

The quantity of spirits in the universe is limited.
In order for a spirit, a ball of light, to enter the body of a
fetus (birth) with a rented soul, the soul of another must exit
a different body (death) at the same time.

All the spirit's past journey is documented in the *Book of
Life,* which located in the *Universal Cosmic Library,* such
as what are the soul's main and secondary lifelines, destiny,
and lessons; in which bodies did it dwell - where, when, and
for how long; from what it had suffered and what knowledge
it gained.

With the help of a medium, spiritual tools, or deep
meditation, you can reveal spiritual messages and
information, regarding your *Book of Life.*

Not all the information will be given to you, in order not to
confuse you, maintain your curiosity, and allow you to have
free will.

A spiritual guide

You cannot be alone on Earth. Each soul in a physical body and every living being has one spiritual guide or more. The role of the spiritual guide is to provide guidance regarding decisions in the person's life. ***The Creation* provides this spiritual guidance for every living body that contains a soul on the physical dimensions in the universe.**

A spirit may incarnate as a plant, an animal, human being, alien, entity of light, and more.

A spirit's travels can go up or down the spiritual hierarchy.

In your current incarnation you are a human being, but in your next incarnations, you might be an animal (lower frequency), or an entity (higher frequency). It depends on which lessons you accomplished in your past incarnations.

During a person's lifetime, the spiritual guide changes every several years, depending on the help that the person needs. While the spiritual guides change, people might temporarily feel uncertainty, loneliness, depression, etc.

A spiritual guide usually does not know you from previous or current incarnations, but might be a departed family member or a friend from the past, or a historical figure.

A spiritual guide does not reveal himself to humans, because it might scare them, rather than help.

Past life regression

Each person has a subconscious, in which all information about his previous incarnations is stored.

The conscious part of the brain represses the past incarnations, in order for you to remain balanced and not go insane from 'remembering' your past incarnations, of which some were good and others not, and to allow you a fresh start to choose and correct without feelings of guilt.

When people are afraid or feel threatened by something in their lives, it means that their subconscious 'remembers' a similar encounter from a previous incarnation, an encounter which has left its mark of trauma, fear, and frustration, which affects them in their current life.

This is similar to when people feel an attachment to or detachment from certain people, interests, professions, places, objects, animals, etc. This means that their subconscious 'remembers' a similar encounter, negative or positive from their previous life. There are no coincidences.

All past incarnations are stored in the subconscious of the person. As much as there were good experiences, there were also bad experiences, traumas, and horrible experiences, which are hidden from the conscience, in order to allow a fresh start without remembering the past. That is why you have to be extremely cautious regarding **past life regression.**

If you choose to do a past life regression, please remember that you can't correct the images from your previous incarnations, but can only change your perspective and understanding. All that happened for a short period of time and for your own good.

Many spiritual advisors don't have the right knowledge and experience to handle the delicate and vulnerable information from the past life regression, which may be handled in an irresponsible manner and will likely cause the patient damage. Past life regression must be done properly following the instruction and assistance of mediums or healers, who can receive information and provide only the relevant and useful data, without changing the events. They may carefully take the patient back in time with them to see all his past lives. Doing so without professional skills can be risky and might leave fears and traumas in the patient.

"That which is hidden from you
in the subconscious – you must not touch.
There is a divine higher purpose that
prevents you from remembering,
in order to protect you and allow you
to make a new choice each time without
looking back".

The right thing to do is, to turn to a highly-skilled spiritual person or a medium who can see the patient's incarnations, without taking the patient with him into his past, and provide him with answers, without frightening him.

Karma

In Sanskrit, *'karma'* refers to the spiritual principle of cause and effect to every action.

Karma is an impact energy, that the spirit carries with it from its previous incarnations into the following ones, which it didn't complete yet. **Karma is the energetic engine, which leads and pushes the spirit to fulfill and correct itself from one incarnation to the next.**

Every human being is born with a karma to complete, otherwise he wouldn't be born.

If the spirit will not finish a karmatic test in a current incarnation, then it will continue to the next incarnation, and so on, until it completes the karma and ascends to a new energy level.

There are no coincidences. Each person whom you have met, fallen in love with, were hurt by or had an argument with, probably is known to you from your past incarnations and your soul has chosen to reincarnate with that person again, in order to finish karma issues that were not successful in the past.

Most cases of crimes, such as murder, killing, crime, suicide, etc. are the result of negative *karma*, which the soul carries with it from past incarnations and repeats the same mistake, because it did not yet achieve a correction.

The moment the soul finishes the karma, then it will have reached a correction and will not need to reincarnate again with that same person or issue in its future incarnations.

In order to complete its correction, a soul does not need to forgive and love every person or issue in each and every incarnation, but must feel complete without negative feelings of anger and disappointments towards those people or events.

As long as you hold negative thoughts about a person, you will need to pass through more incarnations, as many as you need.

Karma Cleansing

Medical problems originate from the spiritual state. Karma cleansing involves a person's option to clean and disconnect karmas and negative energies from his past incarnations.

Karma cleansing can be done in the following ways:
1. Imagine the troubling person or issue, standing in front of you, face to face, while the umbilical cord is connected between both of you.

2. Imagine yourself holding a sharp instrument and cutting the umbilical cord in the middle.

3. Half of each umbilical cord will be absorbed by each body.

4. Wrap the troubling person or issue with a bubble of any color. Ask the person or the issue to turn around and start walking away, until it becomes a tiny dot of light on the horizon. Begin with telling the other person or issue, your complaints and then continue with the compliments. This can be repeated several times until you feel a relief and change.

Chapter 8:
Auras and chakras

Auras

Every living body has auras that protect and balance it.

Seven auras surround the body
Their purpose is to preserve and protect **the body from the outside.**

Seven chakras are within the body
Their purpose is to preserve and protect **the soul from within.**

An aura is an energetic frequency field, which surrounds every living creature. Each field has a different strength and frequency vibration which can be measured.

Every energy field of the auras is being affected by the physical, emotional, spiritual, and mental state of the living creature, which affect the auras' clarity, wholeness, size, shape, and color.

The colors of the auras are indications of the person's personality, behavior patterns, reactions, inner consciousness, etc.

Types of auras

Following are descriptions of auras, from the inside to the outside of the body:

1. The physical aura - the first aura, the closest to the physical body.
2. The etheric aura - is located second.
3. The emotional aura - is located third.
4. The mental aura - is located fourth.
5. The causal /intuitive aura - is located fifth.
6. The spiritual aura - is located sixth.
7. The divine aura - is located seventh and last.

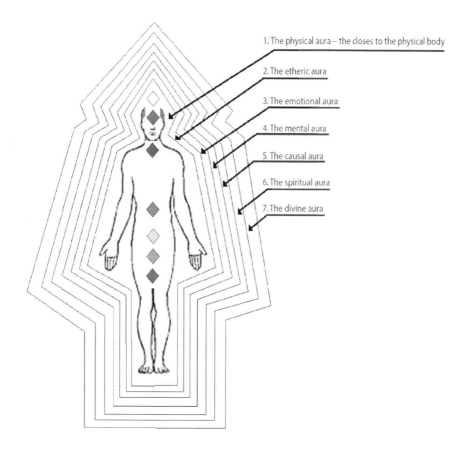

1. The physical aura – the closes to the physical body
2. The etheric aura
3. The emotional aura
4. The mental aura
5. The causal aura
6. The spiritual aura
7. The divine aura

The meaning of the colors of the auras

Nowadays, technological instruments are able to photograph mixed colorful auras which surround a living body, while each color has its own meaning:

Blue: Imagination and inspiration, communication and channeling, intuition and serenity, sensitivity and sadness, memory problems and inner concern.

Green: Care and sympathy, honesty and support, calmness and sensitivity, jealousy and suspiciousness, lack of care and lack of confidence.

Purple: Spirituality and supernatural senses, care and leadership, independence and humility, wisdom and revenge, control and coercion.

Pink: Love and pampering, sensitivity and compassion, care and friendship, humility and beauty, distrust and lack of confidence.

Red: Energy and control, love and joy, passion and sexuality, self-confidence and creativity, jealousy and distrust, power and moodiness.

Yellow: Wisdom and learning, renewal and hate, optimism and creativity.

Orange: Pride and vanity, incitement and criticism, ego and distrust.

Brown: The color of dirt, the source of growth, communication and care, loneliness and vulnerability, secrecy and illness.

Silver: Healing and spirituality, compassion and fertility, high level of creativity, implies disinterest and materialism.

Gold: Healing and inspiration, energy and spiritual enlightenment, disinterest in others and egocentric, materialism and jealousy.

Black: Implies a frightened individual who needs protection and assistance in life or sometimes can represent dark entities. Sometimes there could be holes and cracks that appear in the auras following a crisis, illness, addiction, or abuse.

White: The white color contains all colors, just like in a prism. It reflects purity, creativity, truth, good-heartedness, enlightenment, insight and a high level of communication.

Chakras

The word chakra means an energetic spinning wheels, which exist in all living creatures.
The human body has seven main energy centers, which are connected to the central body lines, from the upper part, the crown of the head, to the lower part, the tailbone, which is at the end of the spinal column.

Between these main energy centers, numerous secondary chakra centers are connected inside the physical body and between the auras. These points are used in acupuncture. **Each main chakra is responsible for a different layer of the body and they all work together, in order to balance the human body.**

Each chakra is associated with different parts of the physical body, with a different color and sound, as all chakras work together and contain the seven colors of the rainbow, which are: red, orange, yellow, green, blue, purple, and white. As in a prism, they are all composed of the spectrum's colors and are arranged by wavelengths.

All seven colors merge into the pure white color of the soul.

Types of chakras

Here are the descriptions of the chakras, from the lowest chakra to the highest one:

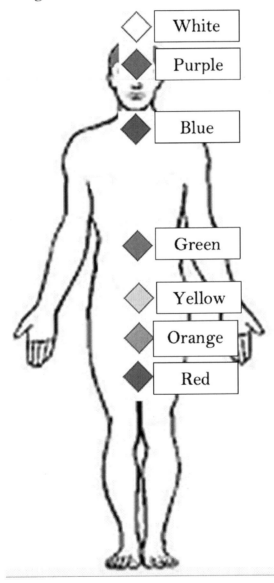

1. Red - The Root Chakra

Located in the tailbone. Base chakra.
Responsible for the survival instinct, success, procreation. It is the source of inspiration and wishes.
Controls the bodily functions of the kidneys, the pituitary gland, lower spine, and feet.
Symptoms indicating that it is blocked: fear, pressure, concern, stubbornness, a desire to struggle and fight, violent tendencies that result from insecurity.

2. Orange - The Sacral Chakra

Located in the pelvis (three fingers below the navel).
Responsible for sexuality and creativity, interpersonal relationships, procreation, courage, fear, desire, and passion.
Controls the bodily functions of the spleen, sexual organs, and back.
Symptoms indicating that it is blocked: restlessness and a lack of concentration. Problems with: interpersonal relationships, sexuality, fertility, kidneys, bladder, and lower back.

3. Yellow - The Solar Plexus Chakra

Located in the diaphragm area, above the navel.
Responsible for the sense of inner strength, sensations, fears, desires and emotions, such as: hatred, anger, jealousy, and depression. When you scare a person, his stomach is the first area that reacts and 'jumps'.
Controls the bodily functions of the liver, pancreas, spleen, gall bladder, nervous system, and psychosomatic problems.
Symptoms indicating that it is blocked: dissatisfaction, sadness, moodiness, frustration, nervousness, ego, depression, blood pressure, intestines, and stomach.

4. Green - The Heart Chakra

Located above the heart, at the center of the chest. It is the central body chakra, which separates the 3 upper chakras and the 3 lower ones and **balances the whole body.**
Responsible for love, compassion, and a sense of forgiveness.
Controls the bodily functions of the circulatory & respiratory systems, lungs, thymus gland, immune & lymphatic systems.
Symptoms indicating that it is blocked: anger, moodiness, nervousness, stubbornness, and dissatisfaction. Problems with: blood flow, blood pressure, diabetes, capillaries, asthma, immune system, lymphatic system.

5. Blue - The Throat Chakra

Located at the base of the throat.

Responsible for self-expression & interpersonal communication.

Controls the bodily functions of the thyroid, neck, throat, vocal cords, communication, and self-confidence.

Symptoms indicating that it is blocked: thyroid, stuttering, criticism, being judgmental, oversensitivity, perfectionism, cynicism, a tendency to catch colds, acute pharyngitis, and neck stiffness.

6. Purple - The Third Eye Chakra

Located in the middle of the forehead, between the eyebrows.

Responsible for clear eyesight, channeling and sensory perception, intuition, deep understanding, ability to imagine and fulfill thoughts and ideas, supernatural sight, and ability to develop the ten senses.

Controls the bodily functions of eyes, ears, intuition, and sleep.

Symptoms indicating that it is blocked: poor eyesight and hearing, head and ear aches.
Problems with: eyes, migraines, an inability to fall asleep, nightmares and inner struggles that result from a lack of self-awareness.

7. White - The Crown Chakra

Located at the crown of the head. The white color contains all seven colors of the rainbow, as a prism.
Responsible for receiving information and analyzing data from the universe, channeling abilities.
Controls the bodily functions of the pineal gland, upper brainstem, right forehead, and right eye.
Symptoms indicating that it is blocked: depression, isolation, lack of caring, a superficial view of the world, and an inability to experience dimensions beyond physical reality.

Chapter 9:
Preparations for the Aquarius Age

World War II

Following WWI, God / *The Creation* decided to intervene in the events on Earth, to prevent self-destruction of countries using atomic bombs and the killing of 100's of millions. This is why *The Creation* created *chaos* and selected the elements of destruction, which were Hitler and his allies. **The motive was to accelerate the process of preparing humanity towards the Earth's entrance to the Aquarius Age, which will officially begin in the year 2106.**

The result was a six-year world-wide war of *chaos*, during the years 1939 - 1945, in which approximately 50 million people were killed globally. This happened by *The Creation,* in order to clean Earth from evil human beings and corruption, and allow more enlightened souls to enter and populate Earth, because souls must leave the bodies of others, in order for other spirits to inhabit human bodies. Each war is filled with ego and male stubbornness and has no winners or losers, all sides suffer from death and destruction.

Each creation begins with chaos

Creation sets targets – in order to recreate

Chooses the element of chaos and destruction

Allows that element to create death and destruction

Annihilates the element of destruction

Finishes an age / era.
Many souls finish their bodily lives

Opens a new age and brings in enlightened souls

World War II was a result of the frustration of the German nation, which had been defeated by the French in World War I and suffered from massive unemployment and a sense of frustration. This brought about the rise of the Nazi party, which still exists until now world-wide. It was led by Hitler (who didn't die, but fled to Argentina) and his Khazarian Zionists and Free Masons satanic supporters, who weren't Jews, but hid behind the Judaism religion as their shield.

The Nazis served Satan and still do so nowadays, while they are taking part in higher positions in all governments. Hence, they are being executed, because they chose to destroy, with their Satanic plan, all that interfered with or threatened them. In order to accomplish this, the Germans used the following measures:

• Government propaganda, brainwashing, using divide and conquer strategy, spreading hate through persuasion, speeches, and conventions.

• The Nazis took pride in being 'an improved race', which they believed was superior to all others. They established a ruthless totalitarian regime, that took out its frustrations on the weakest levels of society, such as foreigners, Jews, Gypsies, physically and mentally disabled, those who had different sexual tendencies, and regime resistors, who all became prisoners in camps.

• They used these prisoners for building gas chambers, ghettos, railroad tracks, roads, concentration, and death camps, in which the Germans captured and killed their own citizens of Germany and other conquered countries.

• The Nazis purchased with the money of their wealthy supporters, mentioned above, a variety of medical, technological and industrial equipment, cyanide gas, ovens for crematoriums, vehicles, weapons, etc., all in order to reduce population numbers and become the only Aryan race.

World War II came to emphasize the fact that:

Ruin and destruction can result from brainwashing, not only in barbarian and cultureless populations, but also in most cultured populations such as the Germans, who were elegant, intellectual and cultured, possessed advanced scientific technology, and preserved nature and environment. The German regime led to environmental destruction.

Following the second rule, 'Everything returns', a karmatic division affected and divided the German society, as everything you do, comes back to you.

Germans lost the war and were divided in two from the fear that the 'Nazi snake' might strike again. Therefore, one part was under the control of the United States and the other was by Russia, for about 40 years, until the year 1989, when Germany was re-united.

Some Nazi seniors committed suicide, unfortunately only a few were caught and put on trial, and many escaped to distant countries, mostly to South America's Chile and Argentina, as Hitler did under false identities.

After WWII many Nazis were invited by the United States government to work at their facilities, in return for providing advanced knowledge, technology, and information. The Nazis, who worshipped Satan, secretly built the new Nazi infrastructure to rule the world and destroy humanity for the benefit of the evil aliens, headed by Hitler's daughters from Eva Brawn as leaders of countries, such as Angela Merkel (Germany), Theresa May (UK), and Dalia

Grybauskaite (Lithuania), along with Obama (USA), Hitler's grandson from another daughter.

All wars were invented, for thousands of years, by evil wealthy satanic people and families, such as Khazarian Zionists, Free Masons, kingdoms, and royalties, who considered themselves above the rest and 'leaders of the world', up-to these days.

These people follow their evil plan to reduce the population every 100 years, as they are afraid of the masses, which can take them down.

Hitler was sponsored by the Khazarian Zionists who aren't Jews, but hid behind Judaism as their shield, that's why they didn't pay with their lives, as the rest of the Jews.

These people, who don't believe in God, planned, funded, and established the State of Israel three years after the end of WWII, in the year 1948, in order to finish their plan, which they started in the Holocaust to exterminate the rest of the Jews at once, and by that reduce the light and empower the darkness and Satan. **The karma will return to repair the injustice, which is biblical.**

The wealthy Khazarian Zionists and Free Masons, don't believe in God. They planned all world-wide financial crisis and the world wars, in order to reduce population and kill all the Jews, because according to the bible, God asked the Jewish people to be and spread light and knowledge to the world. Once you kill Jews, you diminish the light, and by that empower the darkness and Satan. In the universe, there will always be a battle

between light versus darkness, God versus Satan, which exist in order to provide the freedom to choose.

Israel will become the 52nd state of the United States.

The Israeli parliament (Knesset) will turn over the country's management to the Israeli army (under the supervision of the USA army), which will arrest all the corrupted government members and place them on military trial. Then, the army will turn over the power to the citizens, to manage themselves, by creating many communities. This process will happen in each country world-wide.

The extremism of the Nazis to eliminate the Jews from Europe and the rest of the world was extremely intense, up-to the final days of the war

Not the Khazarians but the Jews carry the light, the gospel to the world and as soon as they are eliminated, then the light disappears and the darkness and Satan takes over.

You cannot die. Although millions of people died in WWII, they had the opportunity to be reborn in a new body in their next incarnation, or to remain spirits, according to what they chose after life.

New age children

Those who were born since the year 1945 onwards, mostly belonged to spirits of 'The New Age'.

After the destruction of WWI, God / *The Creation* decided to establish order and reorganize the world, in order to reorganize, as: *'every beginning requires chaos first.'* All the participants were chosen in advance, from Hitler, to the citizens and the victims, as we are all temporary guests on Earth, with missions from *The Creation.*

All spirits are eternal; therefore, nothing can die, but only change its state of matter, moving between matter and spirit and vice versa. The number of spirits is limited, so in order to bring new spirits into the world, others must exit from Earth.

Since the year 1945, new spirits have arrived with advanced abilities, such as cognitive, technological, patience, and curiosity. Many of these spirits came to Earth from distant planets, in order to change the old world for the better, upgrade humanity, and reduce the technology gap between planets in the universe, as we are entering the Aquarius Age in the year 2106, as I wrote in my other books. Many of those children are referred to as Indigo and Crystal.

The Indigo children

Were born since the year 1945 onwards:

The Indigo Children came from distant planets, in order to advance technology, innovation, and improve the quality of life.

They are inventors and considered to be sensitive, genius, very talented, and competitive people with sharp analytical minds, in several domains, such as high-tech, science, medicine, aviation, etc. They earn money more by using their brain and less by using physical force.

Some of them have difficulty finding a common language with people around them. Thanks to the different forms of life, technological progress will be accelerated much faster than we experience today.

The Crystal children

Were born since the year 1960 onwards:

The Crystal children came to unify society and to change the old world for the better, mostly in education and the fight for freedom, as they are known for being the most rebellious. Lots of these children are labeled as ADHD children and most of them came from distant planets as aliens. They are new on Earth; therefore, they are more curious, because everything is new to them. They earn money more by using physical force and less by using their brain.

In the same way that a crystal stone is clear and does not hide anything, so are they, real, honest, and do not hide anything. Some of them don't like to speak much and others love to fight for the community, rights, and justice.

Crystal children are considered to be spiritual, technical, stubborn, rebellious, and impatient. They love the outdoors, adventures, experiences, travel, water, and music. Most of them have almond eyes and a penetrating gaze, which can read other people's thoughts. Their principles are, 'live and let live' and 'respect the environment'.

The crystal children usually activate most of the 10 senses. Their brain waves actually operate in a different way, for example they can hear or see from afar.

They are fearless and have tremendous physical force. It is recommended that they be protected and be given clearly defined boundaries, so that they won't turn to self-destructive ways.

Also, it is important for them be more social, without seeing themselves as victims, in order to strengthen their sense of responsibility and self-confidence.

They don't tend to be violent, but can become ones out of distress, in cases in which the environment does not understand, respect, or assist them.

The Creation decided to bring these advanced children, as a new generation who cares and will change life on Earth for good, in favor of nature, animals, communication, and unity, as we are entering the Aquarius Age, which will officially start in the year 2106.

The crystal children came:

1. To preserve, protect and heal people, animals, and nature on Earth. Also, they came to teach the rest of humanity about emotions, caring, and tolerance.

2. To change the global education system. These children are mistakenly classified as having ADHD. The old broken system does not understand them, because it lacks the necessary financial means, openness to innovation, and most of all tolerance. The changes they are making can already be seen world-wide, such as smaller classes, individualized or outside learning, new ways of studying, remedial teaching, etc. All these good things were achieved thanks to them.

The 1960's

Take those who were born in the year 1945 and add 20 years, then you'll reach the year 1965. This is the enlightened generation of the 'flower children', indigo and crystal, who sought to bring light, peace, love, change the government's priorities, accept others, and improve future generations following the 'make love, not war' slogan, as was done at the Woodstock festival in the United States.

During the 1960's, the youth were able to bring about positive change, such as ending the war with Vietnam, abolishing laws which discriminated against African-Americans, fighting for equal rights for men and women, etc. They left their mark on the field of technology as well, which has developed rapidly since then.

Parenthood license

Bringing children into the world is not part of every person's destiny, but only a human survival need. Currently, about half of the people in the world are, generation after generation, mostly stuck in poverty, lack of education, crime, struggles to support themselves, and become a burden to society, instead of being beneficial and help advance humanity forward.

In the future, people will need to obtain a parenting license, in order to give birth and raise children.

Having children is not a religious need or a personal destiny.
It's not a God commandment to have children.
Human beings decide to have children from ego, and fear of getting older alone.

In order to receive a parenthood license, parents will be required to undergo a process which involves training, examinations, and both physiological and mental health assessments. These will be conducted by qualified institutes, which will be composed of medical, mental, and highly spiritual professionals.

Only adults who choose to become parents and to create a nuclear family for themselves, will be able to become parents, provided they have been trained and have received a parenthood license, which permits them to bring children and educate them.

A license to have children will be given in exactly the same way as other types of licenses are given, such as driver's license, any professional license, contractor license, etc.

Parents provide the basic rules of behavior
and set examples for their children,
while education institutes expand knowledge,
which can be done independently or in a group,
using the Internet and social media.

Parenthood license will be given to certain couples who are:

- Mature emotionally, with financial, physical, mental, and intellectual ability.
- Compassionate, tolerant, respect others, and who have had proper training and education.
- Composed of either a man and a woman, or of the same gender.
- Willing to receive professional support, with guidance, advice, practical solutions for family problems, etc.

As humanity is entering the Aquarius Age, governments will collapse and will be replaced with public committees and civil communities, without boundaries between countries. In this manner, the parenthood license will be a uniform world-wide license, and people around the world will be able to live, work, and raise children anywhere, while citizens of the society will help each other with love and care.

All human activities have a purpose of receiving love and recognition. Each living being must receive love, in order to survive on Earth.

Re-education

A child who had a difficult childhood, might not have gotten the attention, love, education, and protection, which he needed at the beginning of his life. Such a child, will often turn his anger and frustration towards himself, resulting in self-destruction during his life, therefore he will be offered the option to attend re-education villages for short or long-term period, 50% free of charge. Re-education villages will exist world-wide in the country rural zones and mostly managed by the community. **It is very important to have solid foundations as a child, in order to avoid future destruction by the child to himself and the society.**

Just like a single match can burn down an entire forest, a single untrained parent can ruin a child, children, an entire family, and even a generation.

Unfit parents or harmful environment may ruin a child's childhood, and even up-to his adulthood, by inserting anger, brainwash, fear, hate, racism, incitement, violence, and disrespect for others and the environment. These children might even become criminals during their lives and might serve time in court and jail.

It is not right to think like individuals.
All of society needs to think as a unified unit.

Society's assistance with rehabilitation

The society should not label people as criminals and prisoners. Those people didn't have a positive role model at any time during their lives, and therefore became vulnerable and chose to hurt society back. Rather than labeling them, people should respect and help them to adjust back to society.

Death penalty

While humanity is entering the Aquarius Age on Earth, which officially begins in the year 2106, the frequencies will change for the better, people will love more and hate less, and will be more compassionate and caring.

When a person does not respect the life of others, he disrespects his own life, and therefore his life will be at risk, because everything you do comes back to you.

So, if a person takes the life of another, on purpose or by any accident, his life will be taken from him, and he will choose how to die. Unfortunately, there isn't anything more valuable to people than their own lives.

Only when people will pay with their own lives, then they will care and feel responsible for their actions, others, people, animals, nature, air, water, and land.

Nowadays, most people don't respect others. Therefore, unfortunately, there is no other way to teach society to respect other people, the life of others, and all that is around. They will become highly responsible of any life, which is the most sacred element.

People must realize that they will pay with their own lives for takings the lives of others, on purpose or by any accident, directly or indirectly. **In such way, society will be able to prevent** killings, murders, accidents, wars, and violence. **People must recall that they are united and responsible for each other.**

Who really gives life? God does.
When you take a life that God gave others, then you destroy God's creation, therefore you will pay with your own life.

The Creation operates with karma and this balance affects the universe, as everything you do comes back to you. As we mentioned, in order for a spirit to inhabit a living form, in parallel, another soul must exit another body.

The universal karma means that:
Once you take a life, your life will be taken.
Once you save a life, your life will be saved.
All you do comes back to you, because you are the creator of your life and reality.

Each person creates his own reality, which means that the quantity of people on Earth = the quantity of parallel realities, as each person lives and views his reality from his own mind.

The United States

On one hand, the United States possesses some of the most advanced scientific and medical technologies.
On the other hand, many governmental departments contain lots of corrupted public figures, politicians, lobbyists, and current and previous presidents, who benefit themselves and hurt the public, by cooperating with the long-time corruptions of powerful crooked people and companies.

This crooked governmental behavior intentionally maintains society under constant struggle, such as poverty, highly expensive healthcare and insurances, selling of weapons and alcohol without enough regulation and supervision, shooting of innocent people, high drug usage, homelessness, allowing junk food to be served for students at schools, permitting the existence of unhealthy food and tobacco, spraying chemical pesticide on agriculture land and above in the sky, and polluting, all of which cause health problems to the population.

All the governmental damage above, exists in almost every country world-wide, while government employees earn their salary from their citizens' taxes, yet do not provide the citizens with long-term benefits. Therefore, in the coming years governments will no longer exist, once the citizens will rise and eliminate any corruption for good, as karma.

History

The first ancestors of the European immigrants, arrived on ships to the United States. They did not respect, but rather killed, burned, and destroyed Native American villages and often decimated entire populations of Native Americans and others, who were among the original inhabitants of America.

These invaders, brought slaves from Africa to be their laborers. These slaves were considered to be inferior, because of their appearance and origin, and did not have freedom and human rights. These invaders acted toward them with arrogance, meanness, and greediness, as if everything belonged to them and all must serve them. This attitude continues to secretly exist in our time among various sectors in the United States, and world-wide.

The Creation respected and appreciated the enlightened leader Martin Luther King, and sent him to awaken up the African-American people, so that they could attain their basic human rights, as the rest of the citizens in America.

Nowadays, the anger of the African-American people still exists and each racist event may trigger citizen chaos in their communities.

How come people who suffer around the world, from any kind of violence, react back with violence? This cycle cannot end, without turning to compassion and caring for each other.

Even today, many dark-skinned people in the United States feel that they do not belong in America, in spite of their rights and citizenship. This is why they call themselves African Americans, which means that they belong firstly to the continent of Africa and secondly to the United States. Most African Americans feel frustration, as a result of years of government discrimination in education, culture, quality of life, housing, and large salary differences.

Unfortunately, statistically a high percentage of African-Americans and other minorities suffer from racism, poverty, and are uneducated. Because of this, many turn to crime to earn easy fast money.

Each story has two sides, no-one is a victim but chose to be one, and created his own path. Everything starts from education, which leads to a better life. Every person can enrich his own life, based on his decisions and actions. Every person creates his own reality.

Prisons

It is a mistake to punish people who have crossed boundaries and have broken laws, which were invented by other people, and to remove these 'outlaws' from the public eye, by placing them in prisons, which are facilities surrounded by fences and guards, so that they cannot escape. **Humanity does not yet realize, that these people are already in their own inner prison.** Most of them are products of uneducated parents or harmful environment, and many have a difficult life story.

The great majority of these prisoners grew up without education, guidance, and love. Some children grew up to become parents of their own children, who sometime have followed the footsteps of their parents. Unfortunately for most, it's an on-going cycle, which is difficult to pull oneself out of.

It is very easy to manipulate human beings and cause them to behave in certain ways. It's difficult for society to forgive, especially to criminals, who are easily thrown into prisons, as if they were human trash, removing them from the rest of society.

Society tells itself, *"Now the problem is 'solved', these 'problematic' people are in facilities, surrounded with fences, as it is out of sight, out of mind."*

This is not solving the problem, but simply relocating it.

Statistically, a prisoner who is incarcerated, typically does not change his ways and sees himself as a victim, without an option to exit his self-destructive ways. Don't forget that most prisoners do not have other inmates as role models in prisons for them to learn and 'copy' from, and instead they teach each other how to advance their criminal career.

Since when did prison become a solution to every criminal problem?

It is no wonder that the world-wide prison population is in the millions, and keeps growing. Prisons have become the human garbage of society.

In order to end this cycle, you need to educate and provide prisoners with a variety of knowledge, using books, Internet, and society. **God will always give you endless time to change yourself.**

When a prisoner participates and practices in re-education programs while at prison, then his sentence will be reduced accordingly. That will motivate prisoners to correct their ways, in order to be a part of and contribute to society.

When prisoners are released, they will only receive a one-time financial grant, and an opportunity to continue receiving free advice from counselors and mentors, while the society will provide them with job offers, without labeling them. The prisoners' criminal record will gradually be removed from the system, during 10 years, based on their performance. In this way, they will be granted with a genuine option for a fresh start.

If an ex-prisoner chooses to commit crime again, he will be resent to re-education villages, instead of prisons which will eventually disappear as time goes on.

There are currently millions of prisoners in the United States and also world-wide.

Since the 1980's, the number of prisoners in the United States has risen significantly, following the privatization of prisons, which made them for-profit businesses, via the use of very long imprisonment sentences by crooked justice systems.

In the coming years, the power of the citizens world-wide will remove all corrupted organizations, especially as we march toward the Aquarius Age, which will officially begin in the year 2106.

Weapons

The United States is one of the few countries, which allows its citizens to 'protect themselves' by purchasing as many weapons as they like, without enough regulation and supervision, 'thanks' to the corrupted weapons industry, which deals with the government, and uses their lobbyists to gain mutual benefits.

The Creation **encourages freedom, but not the freedom to commit violence.**

Currently, in the United States many innocent citizens are being killed, students go on shooting rampages in educational institutions, certain neighborhoods are not safe to visit, citizens hoard an unlimited number of weapons in their homes, which is like a ticking bomb waiting to explode.

Citizen chaos will arrive in the United States, once the purchasing of weapons will be restricted, up-to being banned.

As we are entering the Aquarius Age, after several years of global struggle, the United States government will change the law regarding the possession of weapons, which at first, will be allowed for those who are in the army and security forces, until they too will surrender their weapons.

At the first stage, citizens will be offered refunds to turn in their weapons, based on the serial numbers on the weapons and the amount on their purchase receipts.

At the second stage, the weapons of the citizens will be collected by the security forces and army, with the aid of robots and tanks. This will create tension and lead to civil war in certain areas.

The fall of empires

Today, most of the countries are ruled by corrupted prime ministers, presidents and royals, who rule based on global evil agenda, as dictators and do not respect the freedom of their citizens.

Humanity is separating from the Pisces Age, the era of corrupted powerful individual men, who have controlled humanity for over two thousand years.

Nowadays, government and rulers control their citizens and force them to obey, mostly by lying to them, using media propaganda, inventing health pandemic, and threatening to take away their stability, security, health, livelihood, property, and children.
As we are entering the Aquarius Age, which will officially start in the year 2106, all humanity on Earth will unite into communities, without boundaries, and will annihilate all governments, rulers, corrupted people, organizations, and companies, as well as the police and army.

People will recall that THEY ARE the power, which was taken away from them, and now the masses will take it back.

Citizens should not be afraid of their governments,

but governments should be afraid of their citizens, because the power is in the masses.

You must unite, rise up, and rebel, in order to create a new better reality for yourselves, your loved ones, and the next generations, because no one else will do it for you.

China

There are over a billion frightened Chinese citizens, ruled by a dictatorship communist government, which does not respect freedom and human rights for its citizens.

Most of the citizens are poor and lack higher education. The Chinese have the largest population on Earth, yet they are the most cowardly and obedient people, who are afraid to rebel, and even assist the government to maintain order.

The Chinese regime is trying to control their people and the world with their economy and money. This regime is afraid of the power of its citizens, who might rebel and overthrow it. Therefore, citizens are not allowed to connect to the world-wide social media networks, but only local ones under government supervision. The regime uses a vast number of policemen, law enforcers, corrupted court, and injects spies among the citizens.

We are entering the Aquarius Age, in which only this Age decides what will happen on Earth, every 2106 years. Towards this age, truth will be revealed, justice will be done, and the power will come back to the citizens world-wide, which will replace all governments with communities, using divine chaos. Therefore, the Chinese people will rise up and abolish all corrupted people, who cooperate with the evil regime.

God / The Creation will destroy half of China by flooding areas with water and killing millions of frightened people with floods and toxic vaccines.

Therefore, large regions of China will be covered with water, until it will sink under the sea, because everything you do, comes back to you. Hence, the karma is arriving fast, as we are reaching the fast Aquarius Age.

Summary words

Dear readers,

For further reading, you are welcome to read my four other books, which were also channeled through me by *The Creation Entities,* and I typed them directly into the computer:

1. The Aquarius Age:

offers the readers with information as humanity is separating from the Pisces Age and entering the incoming Aquarius Age, which is affected by the Zodiac's movement on Earth. The signs of this new age: revealing the truth, fast justice, power returning to the masses, replacing governments with communities, revolutions led mostly by women, and creating heaven on Earth.

2. The Future: Based on the Ages theory

provides the readers with astrological and numerological research and information regarding how the Zodiac aligns with the pages of history. In this research, I moved in time 4,000 years backwards and 25,000 years forward, and discovered there is a mathematical pattern, which has allowed humanity to understand what happened in the past and predict the future, according to the Zodiac's movement.

3. Messages From the Mystical Cards:

The book contains 52 messages in the cards, which were received by the author with the help of channeling from *The Creation Entities*, in order to award a message, hope, and sense of help.

4. Lenormand Tarot Deck Meaning: A guidebook channeled through Anne-Marie Adelaide's spirit

Madame Lenormand was a psychic for over 40 years and gained much publicity and recognition in Europe for the advice she gave to Napoleon and his wife Josephine, the leaders of the French Revolution, and the French aristocrats. Upon her retirement from work, she returned to her hometown as a wealthy woman, even wealthier than the king of France. After her death, she didn't leave behind detailed information on how to read her cards.

Hence, in 2014 Gali Lucy decided to contact her, and received simple instructions regarding how to read them. She wrote this guidebook for half a year thanks to Madame Lenormand's permission to channel with her.

The circle of life has no beginning or end, nothing can be destroyed, yet you can only change the states of matter.

You are balls of lights embodied in a temporary material body as a soul, while your actions testify to the nature of God.

As I wrote at the beginning of this book, don't believe the contents of this book, yet create your own truth, because there will never be a single truth, in order to provide you with a free choice.

Take this book's insights as a different approach. From here you can explore and enrich your own life.

I would greatly appreciate reading your reviews of this book on Amazon. The Amazon link to it is available at: www.Gali4u.com/divine-creation.

You are welcome to listen to my frequency singing, while *The Creation Entities* also channeled through me, as it reaches, relaxes, and heals the soul, on my **YouTube Channel** and website www.Gali4u.com.

Author Website: www.Gali4u.com.

Copyright © 2021 Gali Lucy Nadiv

All rights reserved

About the author

Gali Lucy

Medium, Author, and Architecture Engineer, who channels with

The Creation's Entities since the age of six.

She channels through her brain without any additional tools and advises on a variety of topics world-wide.

She gained vast experience and positive reputation for accuracy in predicting the future, both on a personal and global level, using X-ray remote vision ability.

She is the author of the following spiritual books:

1. Divine Creation
2. The Aquarius Age
3. The Future: Based on the Ages theory
4. Messages from the Mystical Cards
5. Lenormand Tarot Deck Meaning: A guidebook channeled through Anne-Marie Adelaide's spirit

These books were dictated to her through channeling with an easy and simple explanation and information, regarding what is *The Creation's* plan for humanity on planet Earth and to prepare mankind into the entrance of the Aquarius Age.

Printed in Great Britain
by Amazon

30625981R00104